Hello, English
English for Teachers of Children

Chizuko Aiba
Machiko Fujiwara
Brian Byrd
Jason Barrows

音声ファイルのダウンロード／ストリーミング

CD マーク表示がある箇所は、音声を弊社 HP より無料でダウンロード／ストリーミングすることができます。トップページのバナーをクリックし、書籍検索してください。書籍詳細ページに音声ダウンロードアイコンがございますのでそちらから自習用音声としてご活用ください。

https://www.seibido.co.jp

Hello, English
―English for Teachers of Children―

Copyright ©2016 by Chizuko Aiba, Machiko Fujiwara, Brian Byrd, Jason Barrows

音楽提供
©EDUPORT from *26 FUN SONGS*
(*Seven Steps* / *Head, Shoulders, Knees, and Toes* / *Morning Glories*)
©AKASHI, Hayata ©HARIO

All rights reserved for Japan.
No part of this book may be reproduced in any form
without permission from Seibido Co., Ltd.

は し が き

　本書は、将来、小学校教員、幼稚園教員、児童英語講師などを目指す大学生・短大生・専門学校生向けの総合英語テキストです。教育学部、児童学科などに所属する方を中心に、英語を教えることに興味を持つ、幅広い方を対象として想定しています。

　小学校における外国語（英語）教育の機会が増える中、教員を目指すすべての人が、英語でコミュニケーションを図る力、また、実際に授業を行うために必要な知識や技術を身につけることが、ますます必要になっています。同時に、幼稚園や保育園など、低年齢からの英語教育への関心も高まっています。

　本書は、小学校の英語教育、児童英語教育に特化した、ESP (English for Specific Purpose) のテキストも兼ねています。実践的な場面・内容であること、学習者にとって定着しやすい英語であること、現場で必要な知識が得られることなどを基本とし、実践的な英語力をバランスよく育成できるよう配慮しました。

　架空のある小学校・幼稚園を舞台とし、ALT（外国語指導助手）と学級担任がコミュニケーションをとる場面、実際の授業や学校生活における具体的な活動や場面が取り上げられています。まだ教育現場で教えたことのない方も、本書を通じて学校の様子が身近に感じられることでしょう。

　本書には以下のような特長があります。
- ALTと教員・児童との会話を通じて、場面に応じたALTとのコミュニケーションが学べます。
- 基本的な活動や指導法など、すぐに教育現場で使える内容が盛り込まれています。
- 小学校や幼稚園で必要な語彙と教室英語が紹介されています。
- 他教科を英語で学ぶCLIL（内容言語統合型学習）的な実践が紹介されています。
- 日本の文化を紹介する活動などを通じ、児童にグローバルな感覚をもって指導する方法が学べます。
- 英語を通じて、小学校の教育現場に関する基礎的な知識も得ることができます。

　本書を一冊終えたとき、ある程度、子どもへの英語の教え方や工夫の仕方がわかり、臆せずに児童の前に立てるようになることが期待されます。

　本書は、私どもが教育現場で実践・経験したことを基に作成しており、現職教員の研修用テキストとしても、参考にしていただくこともできると考えています。実践のすべてをカバーすることは到底できませんが、教員養成、そして将来の実践の場で、本書が役立つことを願っています。

　最後になりましたが、本書の出版にあたり、ご尽力いただきました株式会社成美堂社長佐野英一郎氏、小学校英語教育の専門的な観点から、企画から編集まで丁寧な仕事をしてくださった井上美佐子氏に感謝申し上げます。また、お力添えをいただきました宍戸真先生、ご助言を賜りました大庭裕先生、ご協力をいただきました出水純二、藤原孝堂、Carmen Willfordの三氏にこの場をお借りしてお礼を申し上げます。

筆者一同

本書の構成と各セクションのねらい

本書は、主に小学校での1年間を想定し、「ALTとの出会いから授業スタートまで」「授業の実際」「他教科を取り入れた英語学習（CLIL）」「学校行事の場面」と4つのパートから成り、合計15ユニットを通して学びます。各ユニットは以下のような構成になっています。

● Dialogue
小学校や幼稚園などの教育現場で教員・ALT・児童が交わす会話表現に慣れ、口頭で練習し、表現を身につけることが目的です。音声を聞いて空欄を埋めるリスニング問題、語句を入れ替えて行う口頭練習があります。

● Listening
各ユニットのトピックに沿った内容を聞き取り、理解することを目的としています。ナレーション形式か、会話形式で構成されています。情報を聞き取れているか、True/False の問題で確認します。

● Column
小学校教員や幼稚園教員が知っておきたい、英語や英語指導についての基本知識、異文化理解に関する知識など、役に立つ情報を得ることができます。

● Reading
トピックに沿った内容などが、200語程度の比較的やさしい英文で書かれています。英文を読み、内容を理解することが目的です。本文に出てくる語句の10個を日本語で確認してから、内容理解に進みます。選択問題に答えながら、内容把握ができているか確認できます。語句は、主に「JACET 8000*」のレベル2～5の範囲のもの、各トピックで知っていた方がよいと思われるものが含まれています。

● Grammar Point
Reading に出てくる基本的な文法項目を選び、文法の理解度を確認することが目的です。日本語に合うように英文を完成させ、理解しているかを確認できます。簡単な解説もあり、理解の助けになるようにしています。

● Topic
学校生活や授業に関連した表現や語彙などを学び、英語で言えるようになることが目的です。イラストと英語や日本語と英語のマッチングなどで問題を解いていきます。多くのユニットで、リズムに乗って語彙や表現を練習できるチャンツを収録しています。ぜひ活用し、音声と一緒に繰り返しながら覚えるようにしましょう。

● Useful Expressions
小学校や幼稚園でよく使われる表現を覚え、使えるようになることが目的です。日本語に合った英文の一部を、語句を並べ替えて完成させる形式です。現場ですぐに使える表現ですので、しっかり覚えましょう。

※本書の表記および音声は、アメリカ英語を使用しています。
*JACET 8000：大学英語教育学会（JACET）が、日本人が国際コミュニケーションを行う上で必要な語彙8,000語を選定したもの。

小学校外国語教育　知っておきたい基礎知識
（1）近年の外国語教育の変遷

■小学校外国語活動

　2002年から、「総合的な学習の時間」の一環として、公立小学校で英語活動が行われるようになりました。その後、2011年度から、小学校高学年で週1コマの「外国語活動」が必修となり、文部科学省作成の児童用テキストやデジタル教材が学校に配付され、用いられてきました。1〜4年生でも、「総合的な学習の時間」や余剰時間を使って、英語にふれる授業を行ってきた学校も多数ありました。

　外国語活動では、基本的な英語の音声や表現にふれながら、積極的にコミュニケーションを図ろうとする態度を育成することを目標に授業が行われてきました。授業計画や授業実施の中心を担ってきたのは学級担任です。学級担任には、「学習者のモデル」として積極的に英語を使うことが求められ、ALT（外国語指導助手）や、ICTを含む視聴覚教材を活用して授業が行われてきました。なお、外国語活動においてはテストや評定はなく、評価は記述式で行われています。

■小学校英語必修化・教科化

　2013年12月に文部科学省より「グローバル化に対応した英語教育改革実施計画」が公表されました。その後の有識者会議等を経て、2020年度から、小学校の外国語教育を高学年で正式教科化し、週2コマ程度、年間70単位時間程度を確保すること、「聞くこと」「話すこと」に加え、「読むこと」「書くこと」も取り入れること、また、中学年では外国語活動を週1コマ程度実施することが示されました。

　2016年度中に新しい学習指導要領が告示され、2018年度より先行実施されました。2020年度から新学習指導要領が全面実施となり、小学校3・4年生では外国語活動が必修化され、小学校5・6年生では英語が教科化されました。教科になることで、教科書が使用され、通知表に成績がつくようになりました。4技能5領域「話す（やり取り）」「話す（発表）」「聞く」「読む」「書く」をバランスよく習得していくことが目標になっています。

　小学校から高等学校までの英語教育を通じて、「英語を使って何ができるようになるか」という観点から目標を設定し、「使える英語力」を育てることが求められています。

■先生を目指す人はどんな準備をすればよいのですか。

　英語が正式教科になると、高学年では、学級担任が専門性を高めて指導するとともに専科教員やALTを活用すること、中学年の外国語活動では、ALT等を活用し、学級担任が中心に授業を行う方針が示されています。

　専科教員やALTの配置は自治体により異なりますので、先生を目指す人は誰でも、英語を指導できるよう準備をしておく必要があります。

　教員採用試験では、学習指導要領の「目標」「内容」のほか、ALTとの会話文や、実際の授業の場面についての問いも増えています。基本的な英語コミュニケーション能力、教室英語表現、基本的な指導法や活動を学んでおく必要があります。本書を用いた学習は、それらの力をつける一助になるでしょう。

　何より、積極的に外国語を使って外国の方とコミュニケーションを図ろうとする態度が、これからの教員にはますます求められることになります。

［文部科学省のWEBサイトもチェックしよう］

　以下は文部科学省「外国語教育」のWEBサイトです。
　http://www.mext.go.jp/a_menu/kokusai/gaikokugo/index.htm

（文責：編集部）

Table of Contents

PART 1　出会いから授業スタートまで

UNIT 1 ALT's First Visit to Minami Elementary School 8
　■ ALT の南小学校への初訪問

UNIT 2 Getting to Know Each Other 14
　■ ALT とのコミュニケーション――互いに知り合う

UNIT 3 School Lunch 20
　■ 学校給食

UNIT 4 Play Time 26
　■ 休み時間

PART 2　授業の実際

UNIT 5 The First English Class 34
　■ 最初の授業

UNIT 6 Teaching Numbers 1 40
　■ 授業スタート（数を教える 1）

UNIT 7 Teaching Numbers 2 46
　■ 授業の展開（数を教える 2）

UNIT 8 Reflection 52
　■ 授業を終える（振り返り）

UNIT 9 Activities at a Kindergarten 58
　■ 幼稚園でのアクティビティ

PART 3　他教科を取り入れた英語学習（CLIL）

UNIT 10 Growing Plants & Observing the Butterfly Lifecycle 66
　■ 朝顔の栽培とチョウの一生――生活科・理科を取り入れて

UNIT 11 Making *Onigiri* and Curry 72
　■ おにぎりとカレーの作り方――家庭科を取り入れて

UNIT 12 Making a Town Map 78
　■ タウンマップを作ろう――社会科を取り入れて

PART 4　学校行事の場面

UNIT 13 Introducing Japanese Culture 86
　■ 日本文化の紹介

UNIT 14 Evacuation Drills 92
　■ 避難訓練

UNIT 15 Graduation 98
　■ 卒業

参考資料
- 小学校外国語教育　知っておきたい基礎知識 (1) (2) (3) ……………… 5, 32, 64
- 小学校での CLIL の実践例（実際の授業の様子より）……………………… 84
- 児童英語教育の定番教材例—マザーグース・歌、絵本— ………………… 104
- 文字指導・フォニックス指導 ………………………………………………… 105
- 学校生活に関わる語彙リスト（科目、クラブ名、学校行事など）………… 106
- 覚えておきたい教室英語表現 50 ……………………………………………… 108

主な登場人物

斉藤祐太
南小学校の外国語（英語）担当。6 年生の学級担任で 28 歳。大学時代の海外旅行がきっかけで、外国の人と話すことが好きになった。

Katherine Smith　キャサリン・スミス（ケイティ）
JET プログラム (p. 9) で来日した ALT。アメリカ合衆国（以下米国）出身の 23 歳。今年度から南小学校に勤めることになった。学生時代に訪日の経験がある。

戸田優子
南小学校の 3 年生の学級担任。30 歳。

Andrew Lopez　アンドリュー・ロペス（アンディ）
JET プログラムで来日した ALT で、フィリピン共和国出身。26 歳。

南小学校
都内にある小学校。英語教育に力を入れており、全学年で英語の時間がある。オーストラリアの子どもたちとの交流や、他教科の内容を英語の授業に取り入れる実践など、さまざまな試みをしている。

 # ALT's First Visit to Minami Elementary School

南小学校に、新しい外国語指導助手（ALT*）のキャサリン・スミス（以下ケイティ*）が打ち合わせのためにやってきました。学校の外国語（英語）担当の斉藤祐太先生が出迎えます。

＊Assistant Language Teacher
＊JETプログラム（右ページ下コラム参照）で派遣されるALTは若者が多いこともあり、小学校では親しみを込めて「ケイティ」または「ケイティ先生」のようにファースト・ネームを用いて呼ぶことが多いようです。本書では現状に沿ってファースト・ネームを使用しています。

 Dialogue

斉藤先生とケイティの初対面の挨拶の場面です。内容を考えながら聞きましょう。

◆ **Listen, Fill in & Repeat** 03

会話を聞いて空欄を埋めましょう。意味を確認し、英語を練習しましょう。

Mr. Saito:	Hello. My name is Saito Yuta*. I'm in (　　　　) of the English classes. Nice to meet you.
Katie:	Nice to meet you, too. My name is <u>Katherine Smith</u>[1]. Please call me <u>Katie</u>[2].
Mr. Saito:	OK, <u>Katie</u>[2]. What (　　　　) our students call you?
Katie:	Please have them call me <u>Katie</u>[2].
Mr. Saito:	OK. I hope you'll enjoy teaching at our school.
Katie:	I'm (　　　　) forward to it.

＊中学校外国語科の検定教科書において、現在、日本人の名前は「姓名」の順で表記されており、本書もこれにならっています。

◆ **Substitution Drill**

上のダイアログの下線部に以下の語句を入れ替え、ペアで練習しましょう。

1	Andrew Lopez	Megan White
2	Andy	Meg

＊英語圏で使われる伝統的な名前には、多くの場合、このように短縮形があります。

UNIT 1: ALT's First Visit to Minami Elementary School

 Listening

斉藤先生は、ケイティに時間割を見せながら、学校や授業について説明をします。児童数、各学年の英語の授業のコマ数、最初の授業の内容などに気をつけて聞きましょう。

◆ True or False 04

内容と一致するものは T (True)、異なるものは F (False) にチェック ☑ しましょう。

　　　　　　　　　　　　　　　　　　　　　　　　　　　　　T　F

1. The school has over 300 students. ☐ ☐

2. Students in the third and fourth grades have English twice a week. ☐ ☐

3. Katie will introduce herself in her first lesson next Tuesday. ☐ ☐

Column　ALT（外国語指導助手）: Assistant Language Teacher

　小学校から高等学校において、日本人教員を補助する立場で語学指導を行うのが ALT です。国の「JET プログラム」（「語学指導等を行う外国青年招致事業」: The Japan Exchange and Teaching Program）により学校に派遣されるほか、自治体の独自採用、ALT の派遣会社等から派遣される場合もあり、雇用形態によって、授業や学校生活への関わり方も異なります。一般的には、日本の教員免許がないと単独で授業はできません。ALT には、授業計画や授業実施で教員を助ける役割が期待されます。また、音声面でのお手本、子どもが英語を使う対象、異文化の伝道者などの役割も担っています。ALT を仲間として迎え、積極的にコミュニケーションをとり信頼関係をつくることが、よい授業のために必要であり、子どもにとってもよいお手本になると言えるでしょう。

斉藤先生は、学校からのお知らせをケイティに渡しました。学校生活について読みましょう。

◆ Word Match　　　CD 05

以下の語句の意味を下の日本語から選び、記号を書きましょう。

1. appropriately [e]　2. indoor shoes [ ]　3. shoebox [ ]
4. entrance hall [ ]　5. briefly [ ]　6. dismissal [ ]　7. recess [ ]
8. period [ ]　9. hallway [ ]　10. teaching materials [ ]

| a. (学校の) 時限 | b. 簡単に | c. 廊下 | d. 教材 | e. 適切に |
| f. 上履き | g. 靴箱 | h. 休み時間 | i. 下校 | j. 玄関ホール |

CD 06

School Information for Ms. Smith

- Please come to school by 8:20 a.m. Call the school if you are late or absent for any reason.
- Please dress appropriately for school.
- Please bring indoor shoes to wear while in the school building. There is a shoebox with your name on it in the entrance hall.
- When you arrive at school, please talk briefly with the homeroom teachers about the day's lessons.
- You will have a meeting with Mr. Saito and some of the homeroom teachers after school on Tuesdays to plan the following week's lessons.
- The first class starts at 8:50 a.m. Each class is 45 minutes long. There are five or six classes a day. The sixth class finishes at 3:15 p.m. and students' dismissal time is 3:40 p.m.
- There is a five-minute break between classes and 20-minute recesses between the second and third periods and after lunch. Students will be happy if you can join them during recesses.
- There is a cleaning time right after lunch. Students take responsibility for cleaning their classrooms, along with the hallways and stairs.
- The English teaching materials are in the cabinet behind your desk.

◆ Comprehension Check

左の英文に関する質問の答えを a 〜 c の中から選びましょう。

1. What should Katie do if she can't come to school?
    a. She should send an email to the school.
    b. She should call the school.
    c. She should send a letter to the school.

2. What will the teachers discuss after school on Tuesdays?
    a. They will discuss the lessons of the day.
    b. They will discuss the following week's lessons.
    c. They will discuss the lessons of the year.

3. Where are the teaching materials?
    a. They are next to Mr. Saito's desk.
    b. They are in the entrance hall.
    c. They are in the cabinet behind Katie's desk.

Grammar Point

（　）内の適切な語句を選び、日本語に合う英文を完成させましょう。

1. 毎朝1時間目は8時50分に始まりますが、明日は8時55分に始まります。
    The first class (will start / starts) at 8:50 a.m. every morning, but it (will start / starts) at 8:55 a.m. tomorrow.

2. 教材を教室に置きっぱなしにしてはいけません。正しい場所に戻して下さい。
    (Please leave / Don't leave) teaching materials in the classroom. (Please return / Don't return) them to the proper place.

> ［現在形・未来形］現在の状態やくり返し行われる動作は、動詞の現在形を使い、未来の予定や行動を表すときは will ＋動詞の原形を使います。
> ［命令文］「〜しなさい」という意味の、命令や要求などの表現では冒頭に動詞の原形を用います。また、文頭や文尾に please（お願いします）を入れると依頼の表現に、文頭に Don't（〜しないで）をつけると禁止の表現になります。

Topic 1: Teachers and Staff

教職員の名称について学びましょう。

◆ Word Match & Chant   CD 07

以下の日本語に合った英語を下から選び、数字を書きましょう。次に音声を聞いて練習しましょう。

- **a.** 校長（　） **b.** 主幹教諭（　） **c.** 司書教諭（　）
- **d.** 図工専科教員（　） **e.** 副校長（　） **f.** 栄養教諭（　）
- **g.** 学級担任（　） **h.** 学校用務員（　） **i.** 教頭（　）
- **j.** 事務職員（　） **k.** 養護教諭（　） **l.** 学童擁護員（　）

① principal　② vice principal　③ head teacher　④ chief teacher
⑤ homeroom teachers (1st, 2nd, 3rd, 4th, 5th, 6th grade teacher)
⑥ art teacher　⑦ music teacher　⑧ nurse teacher
⑨ librarian teacher　⑩ school counselor　⑪ nutrition educator
⑫ office staff　⑬ custodian　⑭ ALT　⑮ crossing guard

＊教職員の構成・職名等は国、地域、学校により異なります。

◆ Practice

例にならって、音楽専科教員、スクールカウンセラーの紹介をしましょう。

This is our <u>principal</u>, <u>Mr. Hayashi</u>.

principal
Mr. Hayashi

1.

music teacher
Ms. Sano

2.

school counselor
Ms. Suzuki

UNIT 1: ALT's First Visit to Minami Elementary School

👉 Useful Expressions

覚えておきたいフレーズを学びましょう。

◆ Word Order

次は新任の ALT を案内する表現です。単語を並び替えて文を完成させましょう。

1. 5年生の学級担任の原先生を紹介します。

   I'd _____ to Ms. Hara,
   　　　　　　　　to / you / like / introduce

   a fifth grade homeroom teacher.

2. 校内を案内します。

   I'll _____ school.
   　　　　　　　　our / around / show / you

3. コピー機の使い方を教えましょう。

   Let me _____
   　　　　　　　　use / you / how / show / to

   the copying machine.

4. ここが教材の保管場所です。

   This _____
   　　　　　　　　keep / where / we / is

   the teaching materials.

5. 何か質問があれば、遠慮なく私に聞いて下さい。

   Please _____ me
   　　　　　　　　feel / ask / to / free

   any questions.

13

UNIT 2 Getting to Know Each Other

斉藤先生はケイティと積極的にコミュニケーションをとるようにしています。会話の様子を見てみましょう。教室の名前や校庭の遊具についての英語表現も学びます。

 **Dialogue**

斉藤先生がケイティに質問をしています。内容を考えながら聞きましょう。

◆ **Listen, Fill in & Repeat** 09

会話を聞いて空欄を埋めましょう。意味を確認し、英語を練習しましょう。

Mr. Saito: Katie, where are you from?
Katie: I'm from <u>the U.S.</u>[1]
Mr. Saito: <u>The U.S.</u>[1] Where in <u>the U.S.</u>[1] are you from?
Katie: I'm from <u>Los Angeles</u>[2].
Mr. Saito: Oh, <u>Los Angeles</u>[2]! I have (　　　　　) there once.
Katie: Oh, really? How did you like it there?
Mr. Saito: I liked it there very much. Where (　　　　　) you live now?
Katie: I live in Asakusa.
Mr. Saito: Oh, it's not far from our school. How do you (　　　　　) to school?
Katie: I come here <u>by bus</u>[3].

UNIT 2: Getting to Know Each Other

◆ Substitution Drill

左のダイアログの下線部に、以下の語句を入れ替え、練習をしましょう。

1	the Philippines*	Australia
2	Manila	Sydney
3	by train	on foot

＊正式名は Republic of the Philippines

 Listening

斉藤先生は、ケイティに学校の見取り図を見せ、各教室の場所について説明しています。何階にどんな教室があるのか、気をつけて聞きましょう。

◆ True or False   CD 10

内容と一致するものは T (True)、異なるものは F (False) にチェック ✓ しましょう。

	T	F
1. The art room and science room are on the first floor.	☐	☐
2. The third and fourth grade classrooms are on the third floor.	☐	☐
3. The library and multi-purpose room are on the second floor.	☐	☐

> **Column**　学年や学級、階の言い方
>
> 「1年生」は the first grade student(s) / the first grader(s) と言います。日本での「1年2組」などの言い方は、英語で Grade 1-Class 2、あるいは Class 1-2、のように言いますが、英語圏の小学校では、Mr. Brown's class のように、担任の先生の名前を冠して言うことが多いようです。また、階の数え方は、米国では1階は first floor、2階は second floor、3階は third floor と言い、日本と同じです。しかし、英国、オーストラリア、ニュージーランドなどでは、1階は ground floor、2階は first floor、3階は second floor と言い、1つずつずれるので注意が必要です。

 Reading

ケイティについてのさまざまな情報です。家族構成、学生時代にしたこと、今回、日本に来た目的、これからしたいと思っていることなどについて読みましょう。

◆ Word Match

以下の語句の意味を下の日本語から選び、記号を書きましょう。

1. freshman* ☐   2. sophomore* ☐   3. junior* ☐
4. to take part in ～ ☐   5. senior* ☐   6. thesis ☐   7. to apply to ～ ☐
8. martial arts ☐   9. musical instrument ☐   10. World Heritage Site ☐

| a. 4年生 | b. 3年生 | c. 2年生 | d. 1年生 | e. 武道 |
| f. 楽器 | g. 世界遺産 | h. 論文 | i. ～に申し込む | j. ～に参加する |

*主に米国の4年生大学での学年の言い方　・動詞はto ～の形で提示している。

More about Katie

Katie is 23 years old. She was born and grew up in Los Angeles. She has two younger brothers; one is in college, and the other is in high school. She went to a university in California. She majored in music and played the violin with the university orchestra.

In her freshman year, she worked as a counselor at a children's camp. In her sophomore year, she traveled to Europe with her family. In her junior year, she took part in an exchange program in Osaka for one month. In her senior year, she wrote her thesis about Broadway musicals.

Katie has been studying Japanese since she returned from Osaka. As she wanted to learn more about Japan, she applied to the JET program* for a teaching position.

Katie now works as an ALT. She teaches English at two elementary schools in Tokyo. She is interested in martial arts, and in her free time she practices aikido. She is planning to learn how to play the koto, a traditional Japanese musical instrument. Katie hasn't traveled much in Japan yet, but she is planning to visit some of the World Heritage Sites such as Himeji Jo or Hiraizumi.

*JET program: Unit1 Column 参照

◆ **Comprehension Check**

左の英文に関する質問の答えをa〜cの中から選びましょう。

1. What did Katie do at the children's camp in the U.S.?
   a. She worked as the camp director.
   b. She worked as an English teacher.
   c. She worked as a counselor.

2. When did she come to Osaka?
   a. She came to Osaka in her sophomore year.
   b. She came to Osaka in her junior year.
   c. She came to Osaka in her senior year.

3. Why did she apply to the JET program?
   a. Because she wanted to learn more about Japan.
   b. Because she wanted to write her thesis about Japan.
   c. Because she wanted to introduce Broadway musicals in Japan.

Grammar Point

（　）の中の適切な語句を選び、日本語に合う英文を完成させましょう。

1. ケイティはロサンゼルスで生まれ、育ちました。
   Katie (is born / was born) and (grows / grew) up in Los Angeles.

2. ケイティは一度ヨーロッパに行ったことがあります。
   Katie (has been to / went to) Europe once.

3. ケイティは5歳からずっとバイオリンを練習しています。
   Katie (was practicing / has been practicing) the violin since she was five years old.

> ［過去形］過去に起こったできごとや動作などを表す場合に使います。
> ［現在完了形］過去に始まった動作・状態を、現在との関わり合いなどで述べる場合に用います。継続・経験・完了・結果の意味があり、have / has ＋過去分詞 の形で表します。have / has been to 〜は「〜へ行ったことがある」という経験の意味になります。
> ［現在完了進行形］過去に始まった動作が現在まで継続している（ずっと〜している）場合に使います。have / has ＋ been ＋動詞の原形＋ ing の形で表します。

Topic 2: Things in the Schoolyard

日本の校庭によくある遊具の言い方について学びましょう。

◆ Word Match & Chant

CD 13

以下の英語に当てはまる遊具をイラストの中から選び、記号を書きましょう。次に音声を聞いて練習しましょう。

1. slide (　)
2. jungle gym (　)
3. seesaw (　)
4. swing (　)
5. climbing pole (　)
6. horizontal bar (　)
7. overhead ladder (　)
8. sandbox (　)
9. flower bed (　)
10. rabbit hutch (　)

◆ Practice

このページに出てくる語を使って練習しましょう。

- There is a rabbit hutch in the schoolyard.
  （1つしかない場合は、there is a/an を使います。）
- There are two swings in the schoolyard.
  （複数ある場合は、there are を使います。）

 Useful Expressions

覚えておきたいフレーズを学びましょう。

◆ Word Order

ALT から児童への質問例です。語を並び替えて文を完成させましょう。次に、下の [Model Answers] を参考に、ペアで Q&A の練習をしましょう。

1. 何年生ですか。

   What _____?

   in / are / grade / you

2. 何のクラブに入っていますか。

   What _____?

   in / club / you / are

3. 好きな科目は何ですか。

   What _____?

   favorite / your / subject / is

4. 友達と学校で何をするのが好きですか。

   What do you like _____ at school?

   your / with / do / to / friends

5. 兄弟（姉妹）はいますか。

   Do you _____ sisters?

   brothers / any / or / have

Model Answers

1. I'm in the (first, second, third, fourth, fifth, sixth) grade.
2. I'm in the _____ club. / I'm on the _____ team*.
3. My favorite subject is _____*.
4. I like to _____.
5. Yes. I have _____. / No, I am an only child.

＊クラブ、科目名などは巻末資料参照

UNIT 3 School Lunch

南小学校では毎年、新任の先生の歓迎会を行っています。斉藤先生が歓迎会にケイティを誘っています。日本の学校給食についても学びましょう。

 Dialogue

歓迎会の日程や待ち合わせ場所などについて、内容を考えながら聞きましょう。

◆ **Listen, Fill in & Repeat**

会話を聞いて空欄を埋めましょう。意味を確認し、英語を練習しましょう。

> Mr. Saito: We're planning <u>a welcome party for the new teachers</u>[1] next Friday evening.
> Katie: Oh, that (　　　　　) fun!
> Mr. Saito: Can you come?
> Katie: Yes, of course. What time will the party (　　　　　)?
> Mr. Saito: It'll start at 6:30. We're going to <u>a Japanese restaurant in Ueno</u>[2].
> Katie: Good.
> Mr. Saito: We can go to the restaurant together.
> Katie: Where shall we meet?
> Mr. Saito: Let's meet at <u>the park exit at Ueno station</u>[3] at 6:15.
> Katie: OK. Thank you for (　　　　　) me.

UNIT 3: School Lunch

◆ Substitution Drill

左のダイアログの下線部に、以下の語句を入れ替え、会話の練習をしましょう。

1	an end-of-year party	a farewell party
2	a Chinese restaurant in Asakusa	an Italian restaurant in Shinjuku
3	the A-4 exit at Asakusa station	the east exit at Shinjuku station

🎧 Listening

ケイティは南小学校で教えるようになって、初めて日本の給食を食べました。日本の小学校の給食と米国の小学校のランチの違いについて、気をつけて聞きましょう。

◆ True or False 16

内容と一致するものは T (True)、異なるものは F (False) にチェック ✓ しましょう。

                                                T   F

1. Katie enjoys the variety of Japanese food served at school. ☐ ☐
2. Katie's school in the U.S. served food that children liked to eat. ☐ ☐
3. Katie often bought peanut butter and jelly sandwiches at school. ☐ ☐

Column　食事のマナー

　食事のマナーは、国や地域によって異なります。例えば欧米では、食卓で人の前に手を伸ばして何かを取るのはマナー違反になりますので、Would you pass me the 〜？とお願いして取ってもらいます。また、外国でスープやパスタを食べる時には、音を出すといやがられますので注意が必要です。手を使って食べる、牛肉や豚肉を食べないなど、国や地域、文化、宗教により、さまざまな違いがあります。お互いの文化や習慣を知り、理解しようとする態度が大切と言えるでしょう。また、箸の使い方のマナーなど、日本の食事のマナーや習慣を、ALT や外国の人に積極的に伝えると喜ばれます。

日本の給食にはいろいろな特色があります。学校で毎月行われていること、保護者が給食を支持する理由、学校給食の優れている点などについて読みましょう。

◆ Word Match　CD 17

以下の語句の意味を下の日本語から選び、記号を書きましょう。

1. unique ☐　2. well-balanced ☐　3. to distribute ☐　4. nutrition ☐
5. regional ☐　6. ingredients ☐　7. to consume ☐　8. efficiently ☐
9. politely ☐　10. to sort ☐

| a. 配布する | b. 地方の | c. 独自の | d. 礼儀正しく | e. 消費する |
| f. 分類する | g. バランスのとれた | h. 栄養 | i. 能率的に | j. 材料 |

CD 18

Kyushoku—Japanese School Lunch

Japan has a unique school lunch system called *kyushoku*, which provides a healthy and well-balanced lunch for all students. Each lunch is carefully planned, and schools distribute a monthly newsletter. The newsletter includes the lunch menu for the month and important facts about food, nutrition, and health.

Schools serve a wide variety of food, including traditional Japanese dishes, international dishes, and seasonal food. Regional ingredients are often used. This helps students understand the importance of "locally produced, locally consumed*." Students and their parents appreciate the variety of food served in the school lunch system. They sometimes request recipes of popular dishes to cook at home.

Kyushoku provides a valuable, hands-on* learning experience each day. Students take turns serving lunch to the other students. The servers of the day wear white coats, caps, and masks, and work together efficiently as a team. Students learn how to set the table, eat politely, and sort and return the dishes.

The foreign media has often praised this Japanese school lunch system, which means much more than just eating lunch.

*locally produced, locally consumed 地産地消　*hands-on 実践の

UNIT 3: School Lunch

◆ **Comprehension Check**

左の英文に関する質問の答えを a ～ c の中から選びましょう。

1. What does *kyushoku* provide for all the students?
    a. It only provides food that students like.
    b. It provides lunch that teachers cook.
    c. It provides a healthy and well-balanced lunch.

2. What do schools serve for lunch?
    a. They serve only locally produced food.
    b. They always serve traditional Japanese dishes.
    c. They sometimes serve foreign dishes.

3. What do the servers of the day wear?
    a. They wear white coats, caps, and masks.
    b. They wear P. E. clothes and masks.
    c. They wear white hats and dresses.

Grammar Point

（　）の中の適切な語を選び、日本語に合う英文を完成させましょう。

1. 学校はおいしいランチを提供します。
    Schools serve (delicious / deliciously) lunches.

2. 児童は手際よく、みんなで作業する方法を学びます。
    Students learn how to work together (efficient / efficiently).

［形容詞・副詞］形容詞（例：happy / healthy / delicious など）は、名詞（人やもの）を修飾したり補語になったりして、その性質や状態を表します。副詞（例：carefully / happily / slowly など）は、動詞（人やものの動作）を修飾するほか、形容詞、副詞、文も修飾します。

Topic 3: The School Lunch Menu

給食のメニューを英語で学びましょう。

◆ Word Match & Chant 🎧 19

メニューに合う英語を選び、記号を書きましょう。次に音声を聞いて練習しましょう。

1. カレーライス (   )

2. トンカツ (   )

3. オムライス (   )

4. 肉じゃが (   )

5. 豚肉の生姜焼き (   )

6. 親子丼 (   )

7. ハヤシライス (   )

8. 焼きそば (   )

> **a.** ginger pork　**b.** curry and rice　**c.** fried noodles
> **d.** pork cutlet　**e.** rice omelet　**f.** hashed beef and rice
> **g.** chicken and eggs on rice　**h.** meat and potato dish

◆ Practice

上のメニューも使って、自分のことについて答えましょう。

What do you like for lunch?

　　I like _____ .

Useful Expressions

覚えておきたいフレーズを学びましょう。

◆ Word Order

給食の時間に関わる言葉です。単語を並べ替えて文を完成させましょう。

1. 今日の献立は何ですか。

    What's _____?

    menu / lunch / today's

2. 今日の給食当番は誰ですか。

    Who _____?

    today / the / are / servers

3. 昼食の時間です。手を洗ってうがいをしましょう。

    It's _____. Wash _____.

    for / time / lunch   and / hands / gargle / your

4. 給食用に机を並べてください。

    Please _____ lunch.

    arrange / the / for / desks

5. 静かに一列に並んで、給食を受け取ってください。

    Please _____

    quietly / up / line / and

    get your lunch.

25

UNIT 4 Play Time

南小学校の児童は、休み時間をどのように過ごしているのでしょうか。ケイティは、米国にも日本の遊びと似ているものがあることに気づきます。

斉藤先生とケイティが、日米の子どもの遊びについて話しています。斉藤先生が何を提案しているのか、考えながら聞きましょう。

◆ **Listen, Fill in & Repeat**   21

会話を聞いて空欄（各2語）を埋めましょう。意味を確認し、英語を練習しましょう。

Mr. Saito: Do you enjoy playing with the students?
Katie: Yes. Last week, I played <u>*Darumasan-ga-koronda*</u>¹ with some students.
Mr. Saito: Did you (   )?
Katie: Yes, it was fun. It is (   ) a game called "<u>Red Light, Green Light</u>"².
Mr. Saito: Is that so?
Katie: Yes, the rules are pretty much the same.
Mr. Saito: Would you like to show the students how to play "<u>Red Light, Green Light</u>"²?
Katie: Yes, (   ) good idea. The students can use English while they play the game!

UNIT 4: Play Time

◆ Substitution Drill

左のダイアログの下線部に以下の語句を入れ替え、ペアで練習しましょう。

| 1 | *Hankachi-otoshi* | *Ishi-keri* |
| 2 | "Duck, Duck, Goose"* | hopscotch* |

*Unit 9 Useful Expressions 参照　　* hopscotch: 石けり遊び

Listening

ケイティが子どもの頃、米国で楽しんだ "Red Light, Green Light" は、どのようなゲームなのでしょうか。順番とルールに気をつけて聞きましょう。

◆ True or False

内容と一致するものは T (True)、異なるものは F (False) をチェック ✓ しましょう。

                                                                                  T   F

1. The players stand about 10 meters away from "it."
2. When "it" says, "Red Light," everyone moves.
3. The first player to touch "it" wins the game.

Column　休み時間のいろいろ

　英米や東南アジアなどの学校では、朝の休み時間 (recess) にスナックを食べる習慣があり、recess はスナックタイムでもあります。学校でおやつを買ったり、スーパーマーケットなどで小袋入りのお菓子 (school snacks) を買ったりして持っていく子どももいます。日本でおやつの時間がないのはどうしてだろうと、不思議に思う外国の人もいるようです。
　一方、給食や清掃などの係活動は海外では必ずしも行われていないようです。欧米では一般に学校の掃除は清掃員 (janitor〔米〕／caretaker〔英〕) の仕事です。日本では、これらの時間も教育活動の一環としてとらえられており、その意義については海外からも高い評価の声があります。

南小学校の休み時間の様子です。人気の遊びは何か、休み時間のメリットはどんな点かなどについて読みましょう。

◆ Word Match 🎧 23

以下の語句の意味を下の日本語から選び、記号を書きましょう。

1. valuable ☐ 2. unicycle ☐ 3. to chat ☐ 4. physical ☐
5. to interact ☐ 6. peer ☐ 7. to establish ☐
8. bond ☐ 9. to settle ☐ 10. quarrel ☐

a. 一輪車	b. (愛情などの)きずな	c. 築く	d. 貴重な
e. 身体の	f. (けんかを)仲裁する	g. 言い争い	h. 仲間
i. (〜と)ふれ合う	j. おしゃべりをする		

🎧 24

Recess

Minami Elementary School has a 20-minute recess in the morning and another 20-minute recess after lunch. Recess is a lot of fun, and a valuable learning experience for students.

In good weather, most students want to go out and play on the playground during recess. They run around and jump rope. They play tag*, hide-and-seek*, hopscotch, soccer, catch*, and traditional Japanese games like *Darumasan-ga-koronda* and *Hana-ichimonme*. Students also enjoy swinging on the swings, going down the slide, climbing on the jungle gym, riding a unicycle, or playing in the sandbox. Others prefer to stay in the classroom or library and read. When they cannot go outside because of the weather, students stay inside and play cards or board games*, draw pictures, read books, sing songs, play musical instruments, or chat with friends.

Recess is good for students in many ways. They move their bodies and get physical exercise. As they interact with their peers, they also develop social skills. They establish strong bonds, learn to settle quarrels, and use their imagination to create new ways to play. Recess is also a time for teachers and students to become better acquainted*.

*tag 鬼ごっこ *hide-and-seek かくれんぼ *catch キャッチボール
*board game (盤を使って行う)ゲーム *become acquainted 懇意になる

UNIT 4: Play Time

◆ Comprehension Check

左の英文に関する質問の答えを a 〜 c の中から選びましょう。

1. How long is the morning recess at Minami Elementary School?
   a. It is 40 minutes long.
   b. It is 20 minutes long.
   c. It is 30 minutes long.

2. What are some of the activities students enjoy during recess?
   a. They enjoy running around outside or reading in the library.
   b. They enjoy cleaning the classrooms and entrance hall.
   c. They enjoy eating snacks and talking with their teachers.

3. Why is recess good for students?
   a. Because they can study for tests and get good grades.
   b. Because they can get physical exercise and develop social skills.
   c. Because they can leave school and enjoy running around.

Grammar Point

（　）の中の適切な語句を選び、日本語に合う英文を完成させましょう。

1. ほとんどの児童は、休み時間に外で遊びたいと思っています。
   Most students want (to play / playing) outside during recess.

2. ケイティは休み時間に、児童の手助けをすることを厭いません。
   Katie does not mind (to help / helping) her students during recess.

［不定詞と動名詞］不定詞は to ＋動詞の原形の形をとり、名詞、形容詞、副詞の役割をします。動名詞は動詞の原形＋ing の形をとり、名詞の役割をします。動詞には、目的語に①不定詞と動名詞の両方を取り、意味が変わらないもの（like, start, continue など）、②不定詞のみを取るもの（agree, expect, hope, plan など）、③動名詞のみを取るもの（avoid, enjoy, mind など）、④どちらを取るかにより意味が異なるもの（remember, try など）があります。

Topic 4: Games

「かくれんぼ」と「鬼ごっこ」に使われる英語表現を学びましょう。

◆ Word Match & Chant

場面に合う英語を下から選び、記号を書きましょう。次に音声を聞いて練習しましょう。

1. Let's play hide and seek!　かくれんぼしよう！

- ①君が鬼だよ。30 数えてね。（　）
- ②もういいかい。（　）
- ③まあだだよ。（　）
- ④もういいよ。（　）
- ⑤みいつけた。（　）

a. Are you ready?　**b.** I found you!
c. You're "it." Count to 30.
d. I'm ready.　**e.** Not yet.

2. Let's play tag!　鬼ごっこしよう！

- ①僕が鬼だよ。（　）
- ②つかまえるよ。（　）
- ③つかまるもんか。（　）
- ④つかまえた。（　）

a. I got you!　**b.** I'm "it."　**c.** You can't get me.　**d.** I'm gonna get you!*

*gonna は going to の口語表現

◆ Practice

上のイラストを見て、それぞれの場面の表現を英語で言ってみましょう。

UNIT 4: Play Time

👉 Useful Expressions

覚えておきたいフレーズを学びましょう。

◆ Word Order

休み時間に関わる表現です。単語を並べ替えて文を完成させましょう。

1. 天気が良いので、外に出て遊びましょう。

It's a nice day. Let's _____.

out / and / play / go

2. 太郎も仲間に入れてあげてね。

Please _____.

you / Taro / join / let

3. あぶない。気をつけて。けがをしないように。

Watch out! Please _____! _____.

careful / be   yourself / hurt / Don't

4. けんかしないでね。仲良くしなさい。

Don't fight. _____.

good / friends / Be

5. 太郎、裕太を押したでしょ。「ごめんなさい」と言いなさい。

Taro, _____.

pushed / Yuta / you

Say, "I'm sorry."

31

小学校外国語教育　知っておきたい基礎知識
（2）授業づくりと指導のポイント

■学級担任だからこそできる授業とは

　外国語活動の成果として、中学生および中学校英語教員への文部科学省の調査から、「小学校で学んだことが中学校で役に立っている」「積極的にコミュニケーションを図ろうとする態度が育っている」「英語の音声に慣れ親しんでいる」「外国の方と臆することなくコミュニケーションが図れる」といったことが挙げられています。これらは、学級担任が中心に行ってきた外国語活動から生まれてきたものと考えられています。

　多くの学級担任は英語の専門家ではありません。しかし、全教科を担当する学級担任には「他教科での学習内容を、外国語活動に取り入れることができる」という大きな強みがあります（本書 Unit 10-12 参照）。また、児童の性格や得意分野を最もよく理解している学級担任だからこそ、児童が思わず取り組みたくなる、児童の興味関心を踏まえた授業づくりが可能になるという点も見逃せません。

　「外国語活動が学級経営にも役立っている」という声もたくさん聞かれます。英語を使って気持ちを伝え合おうとするコミュニケーションの体験を、クラスづくりにつなげている先生方もたくさんいます。児童の身近なものを教材開発に生かすことも、小学校の先生方が得意とするところです。

　教科としての外国語教育には、英語力は必要になりますが、学級担任の持つ指導力は欠かせないと言えるでしょう。

■どんな英語を目指せばよいか　～視聴覚教材も活用して～

　英語が得意な先生よりも、苦手という小学校の先生が多いのが現実でしょう。しかし、流暢でなくても、先生が一生懸命英語を使っている姿、ALTと英語でコミュニケーションをとっている姿が、児童には将来目指すべきお手本になります。

　英語は「国際共通語」として、多様な国や地域の人々がコミュニケーションをとるツールとして用いられています。ネイティブ・スピーカーと同じように英語を話せることが目標なのではありません。英語を通して、異なる文化や価値観を持つ人々と、気持ちを通じ合わせられることを大切にしたいものです。

　もちろん、英語のお手本を示す機会も必要です。ICTを含む視聴覚教材を積極的に活用すること、また、そのスキルを身につけることも、ますます求められることと言えるでしょう。

■まずは「聞く」、次に「話す」ことを大切に

　外国語教育の入門期の指導において、まず優先すべきなのは「聞くこと」です。十分な「聞く活動」を行うことが、無理のない発話（話すこと）へとつながっていきます。

　高学年で正式教科になると、「聞く」「話す」活動を十分に行っていることを前提に、「読む」「書く」活動も取り入れられてきます。しかし、最初から文字を教え込む、単語を機械的に書かせるといった指導は望ましくありません。

　文法事項を教え込んだり、機械的な練習を延々とさせたり、発音を繰り返し矯正したりするような指導も、学習への興味や意欲自体を失わせることになりかねません。発達段階や興味・関心、実態に合わせて、指導や教材を工夫していくことが必要になります。

■大切にしたいALTとのコミュニケーション　～仲間として～

　小学校の外国語教育の推進に伴い、ALTと共に授業を行う機会はますます増えることでしょう。現場の先生たちの多くが、まとまった打ち合わせ時間を取ることがむずかしく、悩んでいるよう

です。朝の時間や休み時間、放課後など、少しの時間でも声をかけ、簡単な打ち合わせをすることが、円滑な授業にも結びついていくでしょう。

そして、本書でも扱っているように、ALT を仲間として迎え、積極的にコミュニケーションをとっていくことが、子どもたちへのお手本となり、また、よい授業にもつながっていくのです。

■自ら動き、情報収集を

大学によっては、地域の小学校の授業のお手伝いをしているところもあります。また、それぞれの地域では、学校の授業公開や研究発表が行われることもあります。インターネット等で情報収集し、授業を見に行く機会を作ってみると、大いに勉強になるでしょう。

授業でよく用いられる教材・教具

(1) 定番的な教材類

●ピクチャーカード（絵カード）
　言葉の意味を音声と共に視覚的に理解させる教材で、黒板に掲示して導入や練習、復習などに広く用いられる。イラストや写真に文字を添えた A4 サイズ程度のものが多い。グループやペアでの活動用には、手札サイズのカードも用いられる。

●歌やチャンツの音源
　学習する表現や内容に沿った歌やチャンツは、英語表現に楽しみながら慣れ親しめ、定着しやすくなる効果も期待される。英語の雰囲気づくりやウォーミング・アップにも活用される（各 Unit Topic 参照）。

●活動用のワークシート（ビンゴカード、インタビューシートなど）
　英語を聞いて行うビンゴゲームや、好きなものをペアで尋ね合うインタビュー活動などに使われる。教員が手作りする場合も多い（ビンゴカードは p. 50 参照）。

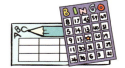

●振り返りカード（Unit 8 参照）

●デジタル教材・オンライン教材等

(2) 場面設定に役立つ教具類

●おもちゃ、人形、パペット、実物など
　パペットがあれば、一人二役で会話のデモンストレーションをして見せることができる。例えば場所を表す言葉を導入する際には、人形と箱を使って、英語表現を言いながら位置関係を示すことなどができる。

(3) 教材として使える身近な素材

●子どもの持ち物、教室や学校にあるもの、チラシなど
　数や色を教えるときには児童の衣服や持ち物、科目や曜日を教えるときにはカレンダーや時間割、国名や場所なら旅行のパンフレット、買い物の表現ならスーパーのチラシなど、工夫次第で身近にあるさまざまなものを教材にできる。

＊準備する機器などの例
　電子黒板、パソコン、タブレット、スピーカーなど

＊参考資料：文部科学省『学習指導要領』『学習指導要領解説』ほか
　　　　　　成美堂『小学校外国語活動の進め方—「ことばの教育」として—』

（文責：編集部）

UNIT 5 The First English Class

6年生の授業に、ケイティが初めて参加します。斉藤先生も積極的に英語で話しています。授業の様子を見てみましょう。

児童はケイティの出身地の場所がわかるでしょうか。内容を考えながら聞きましょう。

◆ **Listen, Fill in & Repeat**

会話を聞いて空欄（各2語）を埋めましょう。意味を確認し、英語を練習しましょう。

Mr. Saito: Everybody, I'd like to introduce our new teacher.
Katie: Hello. My name is Katie Smith[1]. Nice to meet you.
Students: Nice to meet you, too. Where (　　　　　　　　) from?
Katie: I'm from California[2].
Students: California[2].
Mr. Saito: Who can show us California[2] on this map? Any volunteers?
Students: Yes.
Mr. Saito: Kana. Please come up to the front.
....
Katie: Good. It's here. Now I'd like to show you some
(　　　　　　　　) my country.
Students: Good. / Nice.
Mr. Saito: Please use this projector (　　　　　　　　) them bigger.
Katie: OK. Look, there are beautiful beaches[3].

UNIT 5: The First English Class

◆ Substitution Drill

左のダイアログの下線部に以下の語句を入れ替え、グループで練習しましょう。

1	Andy Lopez	Barbara White
2	the Philippines	Singapore
3	many islands	many parks

 Listening

この日の授業の流れについて、斉藤先生とケイティが打ち合わせをしました。1時間の中で、どんな順序で何を行うのかなどに気をつけて聞きましょう。

◆ True or False 28

内容と一致するものはT (True)、異なるものはF (False) にチェック ✓ しましょう。

                                                    T   F

1. The purpose of today's lesson is to talk about Japan. ☐ ☐

2. Katie can ask the students simple questions. ☐ ☐

3. The last activity for today's lesson is self-introductions. ☐ ☐

> **Column**　チャンツ（chant / chants）と歌＊
>
> 　Chantとは歌の詠唱を指す語ですが、英語教育では、単語や英文を一定のリズムに乗せて言うもの（指導・教材）を指します。リズムに乗せて口ずさむことで覚えやすく、英語の特徴である強弱やイントネーションに慣れ親しめる効果があるとされ、児童英語教育では歌と共に広く活用されています。英語のリズムに合った自然なチャンツを選び上手に活用するとよいでしょう。チャンツや歌を使うと、英語の表現や文型なども定着しやすくなりますので、取り入れたい教材です。動作を伴った、チャンツや歌なども効果的です。学年やレベルに合った教材を使いましょう。

＊歌の例は巻末資料も参照

📖 Reading

南小学校では、毎時間の指導案に沿って授業を進めています。1時間の授業の流れについて読みましょう。

◆ Word Match 🎧 29

以下の語句の意味を下の日本語から選び、記号を書きましょう。

1. daily conversation ☐ 2. small talk ☐ 3. reinforcement ☐
4. sentence pattern ☐ 5. target expression ☐ 6. to reflect ☐
7. to praise ☐ 8. to fill out ☐ 9. flexibility ☐ 10. to vary ☐

a. 雑談	b. 振り返る	c. 柔軟性	d. 記入する	e. 強化
f. 目標表現	g. 変化する	h. ほめる	i. 日常会話	j. 文型

🎧 30

An English Lesson Plan at Minami Elementary School

Each lesson is usually planned following a four-step pattern. Here is an example of a 45-minute lesson plan.

Step 1: Greetings and Daily Conversation (5 minutes)
Greet all the students. Small talk such as "How is the weather today?" or "Did you have a nice weekend?" can be included in this step.

Step 2: Reviewing (5-10 minutes)
Review what the students have learned in previous lessons for reinforcement and warming-up. Chants and songs can be used to review expressions and sentence patterns.

Step 3: New Content / Development (25-30 minutes)
Introduce new vocabulary and expressions using picture cards, digital materials, and textbooks. Have students do a variety of fun activities with their classmates in pairs or groups to communicate using target expressions.

Step 4: Reflection (5 minutes)
Praise the students for their attitude and use of English. Have the students reflect on the class by filling out reflection cards* or a Can-Do list*. Finally, say good-bye to the students.

The above is just one example. When making your own lesson plans, allow for flexibility. Remember that the time required for each step will vary according to the activities and the needs of your students.

*reflection card 振り返りカード　*Can-Do list: Unit 8 Column 参照

◆ Comprehension Check

左の英文に関する質問の答えを a ～ c の中から選びましょう。

1. How many steps are usually followed in a lesson?
   a. Two steps are usually followed.
   b. Three steps are usually followed.
   c. Four steps are usually followed.

2. How do the students do the activities?
   a. They never do the activities in pairs.
   b. They always do the activities in groups.
   c. They do the activities in pairs or in groups.

3. What do the students do at the end of the class?
   a. They write next week's lesson plan.
   b. They fill out reflection cards.
   c. They write letters to the teachers.

Grammar Point

（　　）の中の適切な語句を選び、日本語に合う英文を完成させなさい。

1. 英語のチャンツと歌を、教員は復習に使います。
   English chants and songs (are using / are used) by teachers for reviewing.

2. 振り返りカードは、授業の終わりに配布されます。
   Reflection cards (are passing / are passed) around at the end of class.

3. 児童は、振り返りカードにコメントを書いています。
   Students (are writing / are written) their comments on reflection cards.

［受動態］「be 動詞＋過去分詞（他動詞）」で「～される」「～されている」という意味を表します。通常「～によって」と訳される by ～で動作主（動作を行う者）を表しますが、by 以外の前置詞で表す場合もあるので注意しましょう。受動態は、動作を行う側よりも受ける側に焦点を当てる場合、または動作主を示す必要がない場合などに使われます。

Topic 5: Words of Praise

教室で使いたいほめ言葉を学びましょう。

◆ Sentence Match & Chant　　CD 31

以下の2と3については、英語に合う日本語を選び、記号を書きましょう。次に音声を聞いて練習しましょう。

1. **Praise**（ほめ言葉「よくできました！」）

    ① Good job!　　② Great!
    ③ Excellent!　　④ You did it!

2. **Encouragement**（激励する言葉）

    ① Nice try!　　(　　)　② Keep trying!　(　　)
    ③ Don't give up!　(　　)　④ You can do it!　(　　)

    > a. あきらめないで。　　b. がんばったね（惜しいね）。
    > c. この調子で続けてね。　d. あなたならできますよ。

3. **Compliments on the Day's Lesson**（今日の活動をほめる言葉）

    ① Good teamwork!　　　　(　　)
    ② Good eye contact!　　　(　　)
    ③ You listened very well.　(　　)
    ④ You worked hard today.　(　　)

    > a. アイコンタクトがよくできました。
    > b. とてもよく聞けました。
    > c. 今日は一生懸命がんばりましたね。
    > d. チームワークが良かったです。

UNIT 5: The First English Class

 Useful Expressions

覚えておきたいフレーズを学びましょう。

◆ Word Order

授業のウォーミングアップとしての Small Talk の表現です。単語を並び替えて文を完成させましょう（1語、不要な語があります）。さらに、各質問の答えとして適切なものを下から選び、（　）に記号を書きましょう。

1. 今日はどんな天気ですか。（　　）

   How _____?

   today / is / weather / like / the

2. 今日は何月何日ですか。（　　）

   What's _____?

   date / today / the / day

3. 今日は何曜日ですか。（　　）

   What _____?

   date / today / day / it / is

4. よい週末を過ごしましたか。（　　）

   Did _____?

   weekend / a / have / nice / you / on

5. 夏休みはどうでしたか。（　　）

   _____?

   What / was / your / vacation / How / summer

6. 休み時間に何をしましたか。（　　）

   What _____?

   during / you / do / did / recess / after

Answers*
a. It was really good.	b. Yes. I went to Karuizawa.
c. It's October 5th.	d. I played jump rope and dodgeball.
e. It's sunny and hot.	f. It's Friday.

＊巻末資料参照

UNIT 6 Teaching Numbers 1

南小学校のもう一人の ALT、アンドリュー・ロペス（以下アンディ）が、3年生の学級担任、戸田優子先生と授業を行います。数を使った授業の様子を見ながら、指導手順や活動についても学びましょう。

 Dialogue

戸田先生とアンディの授業が始まりました。どのような内容を、どのように指導するのか考えながら聞きましょう。

◆ Listen, Fill in & Repeat 33

会話を聞いて空欄を埋めましょう。意味を確認し、英語を練習しましょう。

> Ms. Toda: Hi, Andy! Everyone, it's English time.
> Andy: Hello, everyone.
> Students: Hello, Andy.
> Andy: How are you today?
> Students: Good. / Fine. How are you, Andy?
> Andy: I (　　　　　) good.
> Ms. Toda: Today we'll (　　　　　) to count to 20.
> Students: OK!
> Ms. Toda: You know the numbers to 10 well. Let's (　　　　　) the number rhyme*.
> Students: OK. One-sun….
> Andy: Good! Now I'll say the numbers from 11 to 20. Listen carefully and repeat after me.
> Andy & Students: 11, 12, 13, 14….
> Ms. Toda: Andy, could you use these number cards[1] and count again?
> Andy: OK. Let's count together this time.
> ………………………………………………………………
> Ms. Toda: Good job! Today we'll play the missing game and number bingo[2].

*Topic 6 参照

◆ Substitution Drill

左のダイアログの下線部に以下の語句を入れ替え、グループで練習しましょう。

1	this chart	these sticks
2	number *karuta**	math *karuta**

*Unit 7 Reading 参照

🎧 Listening

この日の授業の流れについて、戸田先生がアンディに相談しています。活動の順序や内容について、気をつけて聞きましょう。

◆ True or False

内容と一致するものは T (True)、異なるものは F (False) にチェック ✓ しましょう。

　　　　　　　　　　　　　　　　　　　　　　　　　　　　T　F

1. Ms. Toda asked Andy to bring number cards and sticks. ☐ ☐

2. Andy will play number games at the beginning of the lesson. ☐ ☐

3. Andy will introduce English phrases for playing games to the students. ☐ ☐

Column Rhyme & Mother Goose

　Rhyme/Rhyming（ライム／ライミング）とは日本語では「踏韻（韻を踏むこと）」です。つまり、英語の音をそろえる（例：cat–hat、rain–train など）ことで、英語の歌や言葉遊びなどによく用いられます。Rhyme が一定の箇所に用いられリズミカルであることを特徴とする Nursery Rhymes は、Mother Goose（マザーグース）* としても知られています。マザーグースは、英米などの英語圏で昔から親しまれている伝承童謡の総称です。日常にもマザーグースの表現がさりげなく使われていることから、マザーグースを知ることは欧米の文化を知ることにも役立つと言われています。日本でも、子どもの英語指導にマザーグースはよく用いられています。

＊マザーグースの例は巻末資料参照

 Reading

日本の児童が、英語で数字を習うときに間違えやすい点について書かれています。どのような注意が必要かについて読んでみましょう。

◆ Word Match 🎧 35

以下の語句の意味を下の日本語から選び、記号を書きましょう。

1. challenging ☐   2. note ☐   3. little ☐   4. to pronounce ☐
5. to take time ☐   6. while ☐   7. slightly ☐   8. to end in ～ ☐
9. to be confused with ～ ☐   10. extra ☐

a. わずかに	b. ～で終わる	c. ほとんどない	d. 余分な
e. 時間がかかる	f. 一方	g. 骨の折れる	h. 注意書き
i. ～と区別がつかなくなる	j. 発音する		

🎧 36

Teaching the Numbers

Teaching numbers to Japanese students can be challenging, but the following notes will help.

Although most students have little trouble counting from 1 to 10, they need help to be able to pronounce each number clearly. Students grow up hearing English words with katakana pronunciation, so they naturally say words in the same way. For example, "two" is often pronounced "tsuu," "three" "surii," and so on. Once students learn words using katakana pronunciation, it takes time to correct them.

Remembering the numbers from 11 to 20 is difficult. 11 and 12 do not follow a regular pattern. While 14, 16, 17, 18 and 19 follow a pattern, 13 and 15 are slightly different. You will sometimes hear students say "three-teen" and "five-teen."

Once students learn the numbers to 20, it is not so hard to count to 100, but there are some numbers you should teach carefully. Numbers ending in "teen" are easily confused with numbers ending in "ty" like "thirteen and thirty," "fourteen and forty," "fifteen and fifty," and so on.

When you teach numbers, have your students listen carefully and practice saying them many times. You may need to give students extra help with difficult numbers.

UNIT 6: Teaching Numbers 1

◆ Comprehension Check

左の英文に関する質問の答えを a 〜 c の中から選びましょう。

1. Is it difficult for Japanese students to count the numbers from 1 to 10?
   a. No, but they need to learn how to pronounce them clearly.
   b. No, but they need to learn how to count them faster.
   c. No, but they need to learn how to spell them.

2. Why is it difficult to remember the numbers 11 and 12?
   a. Because the students don't learn these numbers.
   b. Because these numbers are not used very often.
   c. Because these numbers do not follow a regular pattern.

3. What numbers are easily confused?
   a. The numbers between 20 and 40.
   b. The numbers that end with "teen" and "ty."
   c. The numbers that follow a regular pattern.

Grammar Point

（　　）内の適切な語を選び、日本語に合う英文を完成させましょう。

1. 来週、児童は 60 までの数字を学びますので、時刻を言えるようになります。
   The students will learn the numbers from 1 to 60 next week, (or / so) they will be able to tell time.

2. 児童は 1 から 10 まで数を言えましたが、はっきりとした発音はできませんでした。
   (Although / Because) the students could say the numbers from 1 to 10, they could not pronounce them clearly.

> ［接続詞］語句や文をつなげるときに使います。and（そして）、but（しかし）、or（または）、so（だから）は等位接続詞と呼ばれ、対等な関係でつながります。それに対して、although（〜であるけれども）、because（なぜなら）、when（〜のとき）などは、対等な関係ではなく、主従関係を作って文と文をつなげるときに使います。

Topic 6: Number Activities

数をテーマにした活動（アクティビティ）を学びましょう。

◆ Number Rhyme & Chant　CD 37

1から10の数と同じ音で終わる語（rhyming word）を、イラストもヒントに、下から選び、書きましょう。次に音声を聞いて練習しましょう。

1. one   – _____
2. two   – _____
3. three – _____
4. four   – _____
5. five   – _____
6. six   – _____
7. seven – _____
8. eight – _____
9. nine   – _____
10. ten   – _____

eleven, shoe, door, tree, hen, mix, sun, dive, line, gate

◆ Song: *Seven Steps* ♪　CD 38

子どもが数に慣れ親しむのによく使われる歌です。音声を聞いて、歌ってみましょう。変化をつけて歌うことで、何度も練習できます。グループ等でも楽しい方法を考えて、発表しましょう。

① 1, 2, 3, 4, 5, 6, 7,　1, 2, 3, 4, 5, 6, 7,　1, 2, 3,　1, 2, 3,　1, 2, 3, 4, 5, 6, 7.
② Let's skip number 3.（1, 2, ☆, 4, 5, 6, 7）
③ Let's skip number 5.（1, 2, 3, 4, ☆, 6, 7）

＊このほかに、2つの数字を抜かしたり、7から1まで逆に歌ったりするバージョンもあります。

UNIT 6: Teaching Numbers 1

👉 Useful Expressions

覚えておきたいフレーズを学びましょう。

◆ Word Order

Missing Game の説明です。単語を並べ替えて文を完成させましょう。

1. カードを10枚ホワイトボードに貼ります。

    I'll _____ the whiteboard.

    put / cards / on / 10

2. 頭を下げて、目を閉じてください。

    Put your _____ eyes.

    head / and / close / your / down

3. カードを1枚取り去り、残りのカードの位置を替えます。

    I'll _____ away, and mix up

    card / take / one

    the rest of the cards.

4. 目を開けて、なくなったカードを当てましょう。

    Open your eyes _____.

    missing / what's / guess / and

5. 正解です。1点獲得。／ 残念、ちがいます。

    That's right. _____. / Sorry, that's wrong.

    point / one / You / got

45

UNIT 7 Teaching Numbers 2

前回の授業の続きの場面です。楽しく取り組める活動（アクティビティ）を通して、英語表現に慣れ親しむ授業の様子を見てみましょう。

 Dialogue

戸田先生とアンディの授業の続きです。どんな活動をしているのか考えながら聞きましょう。

◆ **Listen, Fill in & Repeat** 40

会話を聞いて空欄を埋めましょう。意味を確認し、英語を練習しましょう。

Ms. Toda: Let's play number bingo! We'll use only English.
Students: Only English! / OK!
Ms. Toda: First, (　　　　　　) a four by four grid on the paper, like this.
Students: Like this?
Ms. Toda: That's right. We'll use the numbers from <u>1 to 20</u>[1].
Students: All right.
Ms. Toda: Write 16 numbers, one in (　　　　　　) square.
Students: Is this OK?
Andy: I'll call out a number. If you have the number, (　　　　　　) it.
Students: OK. Let's play!
Andy: OK. <u>Five</u>![2]
Students: I have it. / I don't have it.
　　　　　　………………………………………………
Students: Bingo! / Bingo!

◆ Substitution Drill

左のダイアログの下線部に以下の語句を入れ替え、グループで練習しましょう。

| 1 | 1 to 40 | 10 to 60 |
| 2 | What is 1 plus 1? | What is 60 minus 2? |

 Listening

戸田先生とアンディが、次の授業の打ち合わせをしています。どんな活動を行うのか、気をつけて聞きましょう。

*math *karuta*: 四則計算を使ったカルタ。Reading 参照。

◆ True or False

 41

内容と一致するものは T (True)、異なるものは F (False) にチェック ✓ しましょう。

　　　　　　　　　　　　　　　　　　　　　　　　　　　　T　F

1. The students will learn the numbers up to 60 next week.

2. Ms. Toda will bring a big map to class next week.

3. The students will play math bingo at the end of the class.

Column　授業におけるゲーム的な活動

　ビンゴゲームやカルタのほかに、フルーツバスケットや伝言ゲームなど、入門期の音声中心の授業では、ゲーム（活動・アクティビティ）が多く活用されます。文部科学省の教材 "Hi, friends!" でも多数のゲームが紹介されています。児童が興味を持って取り組め、飽きずに音声や表現に慣れ親しめることが、ゲーム的な活動の一つのメリットと言えます。「単に楽しむ」ためだけの活動ではなく、ビンゴゲームなら、「最後までしっかり聞く」活動ととらえることができます。全員がルールを理解していること、発話を促す活動の前に、十分な聞く活動を行うこともポイントです。ゲームを「習った英語を使うコミュニケーション活動」につなげていく視点も必要です。

Reading

英語の授業でよく使われる活動にカードゲームがあります。マッチング・カードを使った活動について読みましょう。

◆ Word Match

以下の語句の意味を下の日本語から選び、記号を書きましょう。

🎧 42

1. to spread out ☐　2. face up ☐　3. to slap ☐　4. to grab ☐
5. to call out ☐　6. term ☐　7. addition ☐
8. subtraction ☐　9. multiplication ☐　10. division ☐

a. （平手でぴしゃりと）取る	b. かけ算	c. 表を上にして
d. 足し算	e. 引き算	f. 用語	g. 読み上げる
h. つかむ	i. 割り算	j. 広げる	

🎧 43

Using Matching Cards to Teach Numbers

Karuta, a Japanese matching card game, is one of the most popular traditional Japanese games. To play, you need two sets of cards: *yomi-fuda* (reading cards) and *tori-fuda* (playing cards). Spread out the playing cards face up on the table or floor. One player reads the reading card, and the other players compete to slap or grab the playing card. The one who slaps the card first keeps the card. The player who gets the most cards wins.

Karuta works well in English class. To practice numbers, for example, try number *karuta**. To play number *karuta*, prepare two sets of the same number cards for each group. A teacher or a leader calls out one number, and the other students point to or touch the number called. Math *karuta** is more challenging. Prepare reading cards with questions and playing cards with answers. Introduce the terms "plus" and "minus" and try simple addition and subtraction problems. Ask, "What is 11 plus 5?" or "What is 10 minus 5?" When students are ready for more difficult questions, introduce multiplication and division: "What is 4 times 3?" or "What is 30 divided by 2?"

Give *karuta* a try in your own class. Your students will learn English faster and with more fun playing *karuta*.

*number *karuta*　*math *karuta*: Unit 6 Dialogue の Substitution Drill でも既出

UNIT 7: Teaching Numbers 2

◆ Comprehension Check

左の英文に関する質問の答えを a 〜 c の中から選びましょう。

1. How do the players spread out the *karuta* cards?
    a. They spread out the playing cards face down on the desk.
    b. They spread out the playing cards face up on the desk.
    c. They spread out the reading cards face down on the desk.

2. How do the students play number *karuta*?
    a. The players point to the numbers called.
    b. The readers turn over the numbers called.
    c. The students read the numbers called.

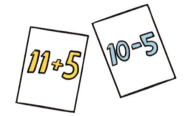

3. Why is *karuta* good for English class?
    a. Because students will learn English faster while having fun.
    b. Because students will learn English slowly while having fun.
    c. Because students will learn English quietly while having fun.

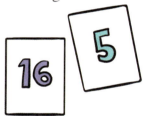

Grammar Point

（　）の中の適切な語・語句を選び、日本語に合う英文を完成させましょう。

1. ほとんどの児童が、引き算より足し算のほうが簡単だと思っています。
   Most students think that addition is (easier / easiest) than subtraction.

2. 小学校で学ぶ四則計算の中で、多くの児童は割り算が最も難しいと思っています。
   Many students think that division is (the most difficult / more difficult) of the four calculations learned in elementary school.

> [比較] 二つのものを比較する場合は**比較級**を用い、三つ以上のものを比較する場合は**最上級**を用います。比較級は原級（形容詞・副詞）に -er がついたり、原級の前に more がついたりします。than を伴い、「〜よりも」という意味を表すことができます。最上級は原級に -est がついたり、原級の前に most がついたりして、「最も〜だ」という意味を表します。一般的に、最上級の前には the を伴います。原級が通常 3 音節以上の場合は、more、most を前につけます。

Topic 7: Words for Playing Bingo

ビンゴゲームで使う表現を学びましょう。

◆ Sentence Match

以下の英文に合う日本語を下から選び、記号を書きましょう。

1. (　　) Let's play bingo! Take a bingo card. Get some chips.
2. (　　) If you have the word that is called, say "I have it." Put a chip on it.
3. (　　) If you don't have the word that is called, say "I don't have it."
4. (　　) One more to bingo!
5. (　　) If you fill in a vertical, horizontal, or diagonal line, say "Bingo."

> **a.** ビンゴをしましょう！ ビンゴカードを取りましょう。チップを取りましょう。
> **b.** 縦、横、斜めのどこか一列がそろったら、「ビンゴ」と言いましょう。
> **c.** あと一つでビンゴ！
> **d.** 言われた言葉があったら、「あった」と言って、チップを置きましょう。
> **e.** 言われた言葉がなかったら、「ない」と言いましょう。

◆ Chant

CD 44

ビンゴに使用する英語表現です。音声を聞いて練習しましょう。

Let's play bingo!　　　　Bingo card, please.
Do you have this word?　Yes! I have it.
I don't have it.　　　　One more to bingo!
Bingo! Bingo!　　　　　I got bingo!

UNIT 7: Teaching Numbers 2

👉 Useful Expressions

覚えておきたいフレーズを学びましょう。

◆ Word Order

英語でカルタを行う時の指示です。単語を並べ替えて文を完成させましょう。

1. カルタをしましょう。グループワーク用に机を並べ替えましょう。

    Let's play *karuta*! Please arrange _____

    the / group / for / desks / work

    _____.

2. カードを上向きにして、机の上にばらばらに並べましょう。

    Spread out the cards _____ desk.

    up / on / the / face

3. 先生が読み上げる言葉を聞いて、カードを取りましょう。

    Listen to the word your teacher _____

    and / calls / grab / out

    the card.

4. 取ったカードを一緒に数えましょう。

    Let's _____ together.

    cards / count / got / you / the

5. 誰がグループで一番カードを多く取りましたか。マリの勝ちです。

    Who _____ your group?

    in / most / got / cards / the

    Mari is the winner.

Tips

児童に定着していない語彙を使ってカルタをすると、わかる児童だけが勝ってしまい、わからない児童は参加もできず、答えの確認もできず、英語の練習になりません。みんなが聞いて理解できるようになるまでは、カードを指差したり (point to)、タッチ (touch) したりする方法がよいでしょう。

51

UNIT 8 Reflection

南小学校では、授業の最後に「振り返り」の時間を持つようにしています。「振り返り」は、児童や教師にとって、どんな意味があるのでしょうか。

 Dialogue

戸田先生とアンディの授業の終盤の様子です。内容を考えながら聞きましょう。

◆ **Listen, Fill in & Repeat** 46

会話を聞いて空欄を埋めましょう。意味を確認し、英語を練習しましょう。

Ms. Toda: Did you enjoy the math *karuta*[1]?
Students: Yes. / Let's play it again.
Ms. Toda: Good. You (　　　　　　) numbers really well.
　Andy: Yes, you worked hard today[2]!
Students: Thank you.
Ms. Toda: Now please fill in your reflection cards. You have five minutes.
　　　　　　……………………………………………………………
Ms. Toda: Are you (　　　　　)? Please (　　　　　　) your cards to the front.
Students: OK. Here you are.
　Andy: That's (　　　　　　) for today. See you next time[3].
Students: See you, Andy.

UNIT 8: Reflection

◆ Substitution Drill

左のダイアログの下線部に以下の語句を入れ替え、グループで練習しましょう。

1	the missing game	the bingo game
2	did a good job	tried really hard
3	next week	on Monday

🎧 Listening

戸田先生とアンディが、今日の授業について話しています。児童の様子や、復習が必要な内容などについて、気をつけて聞きましょう。

◆ True or False CD 47

内容と一致するものは T (True)、異なるものは F (False) にチェック ✓ しましょう。

　　　　　　　　　　　　　　　　　　　　　　　　　　　　T　F

1. Ms. Toda thinks her students did not try hard today. ☐ ☐

2. Andy thinks games make students speak English more freely. ☐ ☐

3. Ms. Toda asked Andy to review the numbers. ☐ ☐

Column　評価と振り返りカード

　授業と評価は一体のものです。評価を通して児童の状況を把握し、教師はそれを授業改善に生かします。外国語活動の評価方法として、行動観察のほかに、児童が自己評価を行う「振り返りカード」が活用されています。授業中の観察だけでは見取れない、児童の努力や気づきなどを知ることで、個別の支援や授業改善につなげていきます。カード記入後に意見を教室でシェアし、先生がコメントを返すことも、児童の意欲を育てることになります。授業のねらいや先生からの振り返りなど、大切なことは、日本語でしっかり伝えることも必要でしょう。なお、教科化に伴い「何ができるか」を示す「Can-Do リスト」も使用されています。

Reading

振り返りカードがどのように使われるのかについて読みましょう。

◆ Word Match 🎧 48

以下の語句の意味を下の日本語から選び、記号を書きましょう。

1. reflection ☐   2. common ☐   3. to respond ☐   4. to aim at 〜 ☐
5. to hesitate ☐   6. to speak out ☐   7. format ☐
8. some … others 〜 ☐   9. to collect ☐   10. confidence ☐

| a. 自信 | b. 振り返り | c. 一般的な | d. 集める | e. …もいれば〜もいる |
| f. 〜を目指す | g. ためらう | h. 応える | i. 書式 | j. 大きな声で言う |

🎧 49

Using Reflection Cards

It is common for many Japanese elementary schools to use *furikaeri*, or reflection cards in their English program. Students respond to questions: Did you listen carefully and try to repeat? Did you try to use the words that you learned? Did you work together with classmates?

Students also write comments: "It was good to learn numbers through bingo," or "I tried hard to use English for the game." Some cards ask what each student wants to aim at: "I will try to use English more," or "I will not hesitate to speak out."

The format, contents, and way of using the cards vary among schools and across grades. Some schools distribute and collect the cards at the end of every lesson, while others do so at the end of each unit. The last five minutes of class time is often used for filling out the cards.

Teachers read the reflection cards and consider how to improve the lessons and make them more communicative. Teachers also write comments to students praising their active participation or encouraging those who lack confidence. Reflection cards thus link teachers and students in the task of learning English.

UNIT 8: Reflection

◆ **Comprehension Check**

左の英文に関する質問の答えをa～cの中から選びましょう。

1. What do students indicate on the reflection cards?
   a. What they think about their school and classmates.
   b. How well they listened to and used English.
   c. What they do in the last five minutes of class time.

2. When do the students fill out reflection cards?
   a. They often do it at the beginning of the class.
   b. They often do it in the middle of the class.
   c. They often do it at the end of the class.

3. How do reflection cards help teachers?
   a. They help teachers consider how to improve their lessons.
   b. They help teachers understand English better.
   c. They help teachers relax after the day's English lesson.

Grammar Point

（　）内の適切な語句を選び、日本語に合う英文を完成させましょう。

1. 児童が授業中にどんなことに気づいたかを振り返りカードで知ることができます。
   Reflection cards can tell (what do students notice / what students notice).

2. アンケートのコメントを読むことにより、教員は児童がどんな活動に興味があるか知ることができます。
   Teachers can know what activities (are students interested / students are interested) in by reading their comments in questionnaires.

[間接疑問] 疑問詞で始まる疑問文が文全体の一部に含まれる間接疑問では、語順が通常の疑問文とは異なり、疑問詞＋主語＋動詞のように、肯定文と同じ語順になります。

Topic 8: Reflection Cards

振り返りカードをもとに、必要な表現を学びましょう。

◆ Sentence Match & Practice 50

以下は、南小学校で使用した振り返りカードの英語版です。英語に合う日本語を下から選んで（　）に記号を書きましょう。次に音声を聞いて練習しましょう。

Reflection Card

Read the questions about today's lesson and circle the number for your answer.

1. Did you listen to the numbers very carefully? (　　)

④	③	②	①
Yes, I really did.	Yes, I did.	No, not really.	No, not at all.

2. Did you try to use the English you learned? (　　)

④	③	②	①
Yes, I really did.	Yes, I did.	No, not really.	No, not at all.

3. Did you notice the difference between katakana and English sounds? (　　)

④	③	②	①
Yes, I really did.	Yes, I did.	No, not really.	No, not at all.

4. Did you try to use English with your friends for the activity? (　　)

④	③	②	①
Yes, I really did.	Yes, I did.	No, not really.	No, not at all.

5. Please write your comments about today's lesson. (　　)

Class: _____　Name: _____

---

a. 学んだ英語を使おうとしましたか。　b. 友達と一緒に、英語を使って活動ができましたか。
c. 数字の言い方を注意深く聞きましたか。　d. カタカナと英語の音の違いに気づきましたか。
e. 今日の授業について書いてください。

UNIT 8: Reflection

 Useful Expressions

覚えておきたいフレーズを学びましょう。

◆ Word Order

授業中にALTに依頼するときの表現です。単語を並び替えて文を完成させましょう。

1. 児童は、あなたが言ったことがよくわかっていないようです。簡単な英語でお願いします。

    The students _____

    understand / seem / to / don't

    what you said. Please use easy English.

2. 児童がクラスメイトと一緒にとてもがんばっています。この活動をもう少し、続けましょう。

    The students _____ their classmates.

    well / with / are / working

    Let's _____ longer.

    this / activity / continue / a little

3. このアクティビティは終わりにして、次の課題に移りましょう。

    Let's finish this activity and _____ next task.

    to / on / move / the

4. 時間が足りません。次のアクティビティはやめましょう。

    We _____.

    enough / have / time / don't

    Let's skip the next activity.

5. 私が黒板にカードを貼っている間に、児童とチャンツを復習してください。

    Please review a chant with the students while I am

    _____ the blackboard.

    on / putting / cards / these

57

UNIT 9 Activities at a Kindergarten

南小学校に隣接した南幼稚園では、アンディをゲストティーチャーとして招きました。幼稚園での活動内容について見てみましょう。

 Dialogue

幼稚園の阿部洋子園長先生がアンディに何を提案しているか、考えながら聞きましょう。

◆ **Listen, Fill in & Repeat**　　　 52

会話を聞いて空欄を埋めましょう。意味を確認し、英語を練習しましょう。

> Ms. Abe: Hello. My name is Abe Yoko. I'm the kindergarten (　　　　).
> Andy: I'm Andy. Nice to meet you, Ms. Abe.
> Ms. Abe: Nice to meet you, too, Andy. The children are looking forward to your (　　　　).
> Andy: Good. What shall I do this week?
> Ms. Abe: Could you teach an (　　　　) English song to the *nenchu* children?
> Andy: OK, I'll teach *Head, Shoulders, Knees and Toes*[1].
> Ms. Abe: Good. For the *nencho* children, please read this book, *The Little Red Hen*[2] and play one simple English game.
> Andy: OK. I'll read the book and then play "Simon Says"[3].

◆ Substitution Drill

左のダイアログの下線部に以下の語句を入れ替え、ペアで練習しましょう。

1	*London Bridge Is Falling Down*	*Twinkle, Twinkle, Little Star*
2	*Brown Bear, Brown Bear, What Do You See?*	*Five Little Monkeys Jumping on the Bed*
3	"Duck, Duck, Goose"*	"Fruit Basket"

*Useful Expressions 参照

Listening

園児たちはアンディに英語の絵本を読んでもらうのを楽しみにしています。今日は *The Little Red Hen* のお話です。何が登場するどんな話か、気をつけて聞きましょう。

◆ True or False　　　　　　　　　　　　　　CD 53

内容と一致するものは T (True)、異なるものは F (False) にチェック しましょう。

　　　　　　　　　　　　　　　　　　　　　　　　　　T　F

1. The little red hen had three busy friends.　　□ □

2. The cat helped the little red hen make flour, but the dog didn't.　　□ □

3. The little red hen ate the bread all by herself.　　□ □

Column　　TPR (全身反応教授法)：Total Physical Response

外国語の入門期の代表的な教授法として TPR があります。1960 年代に米国の心理学者 Dr. James Asher が提唱したもので、命令を聞かせ全身で反応させることを通して外国語を習得させるというものです。例えば指導者が "Stand up." と言って動作を行い、学習者にも同じ動作をさせます。体で反応させながら意味を理解させ、次の段階では指示を聞くだけで反応できるようにします。本 Unit に出てくる "Simon Says" も、この教授法の例です。TPR はまた、授業で新しい語彙を学ぶとき、歌やチャンツの詞の意味を知るとき、活動（アクティビティ）に初めて取り組むときなど、さまざまな場面で用いられます。小学校英語教育・児童英語教育には欠かせない教授法の一つです。

Reading

子どもたちに人気の活動、"Simon Says"の手順です。どのようなルールなのか、子どもの実態に応じてどんなアレンジをするとよいかなどについて読みましょう。

◆ Word Match　🎧 54

以下の語句の意味を下の日本語から選び、記号を書きましょう。

1. ability ☐　　2. command ☐　　3. role ☐　　4. to obey ☐
5. instruction ☐　　6. to clap ☐　　7. to make a mistake ☐
8. to be sure to ～ ☐　　9. according to ～ ☐　　10. to skip ☐

a. 必ず～する	b. 間違う	c. 役割	d. 能力	e. 指示
f.（手を）たたく	g. ～に応じて	h. 命令	i. 従う	j. 抜かす・とばす

🎧 55

How to Play "Simon Says"

"Simon Says" is a popular children's game that is often played in English classes. It helps children with their listening ability, as they have to listen carefully to the commands.

Here is how to play the game. The teacher plays the role of Simon. Simon is a king, and what he says has to be obeyed. The players, however, should only obey instructions that start with the words "Simon says." For example, if the teacher says, "Simon says clap your hands," everybody must clap their hands. If the teacher says only, "Clap your hands," the players must do nothing. Players who make a mistake are out of the game. The last player in the game, the one who has obeyed all of Simon's commands, is the winner. Be sure to use words that students know.

You can change the rules according to each class and age. Let younger children or beginners keep playing even if they make a mistake, or have them sit down and skip one turn, and then join again. In this way, children can enjoy the game without having to worry about winning or losing. For a fun variation, children can repeat each command that starts with "Simon says…." This helps children to speak English, too.

◆ Comprehension Check

左の英文に関する質問の答えを a 〜 c の中から選びましょう。

1. How does the "Simon Says" game help children in English class?
   a. It helps children write better English sentences.
   b. It helps children listen carefully and follow commands.
   c. It helps children read important words and phrases.

2. What instructions should the players obey?
   a. They should obey the instructions that Simon doesn't say.
   b. They should obey all the instructions that the teacher says.
   c. They should obey the instructions that start with "Simon says."

3. What can children do for a fun variation of the game?
   a. They can clap their hands after each command Simon says.
   b. They can repeat each command that starts with "Simon says."
   c. They can stand up after they make two or three mistakes.

Grammar Point

(　) の中の適切な語を選び、日本語に合う英文を完成させましょう。

1. 小さな赤いめんどりは友達に「手伝ってくれますか」と尋ねました。
   The little red hen said to her friends, "(Will / May) you help me?"

2. 「サイモンセズ」では、"Simon says" のない命令には従ってはいけません。
   You (don't have to / must not) obey the instruction given without the words "Simon says" when you play the "Simon Says" game.

[助動詞] 動詞の働きを助ける役割をします。助動詞の後ろには動詞の原形が来ます。can（〜できる）、must・have to / has to（〜しなければならない）、should（〜すべきだ）などがあります。否定形 must not（〜してはいけない）と、don't / doesn't have to（〜する必要がない）では意味が異なりますので注意しましょう。また、疑問形の May I 〜 ? Can I 〜 ? などは許可、Will you 〜 ? Would you 〜 ? などは、依頼を示す場合に使われます。

Topic 9: Body Parts

体の部位について学びましょう。

◆ Practice & Chant　　　　　　　🎧 56~57

イラストを見て体の部位を言ってみましょう。単数形・複数形に注意しましょう。次に音声を聞いて練習しましょう。

① head	② hair	③ face	④ eye(s)	⑤ eyebrow(s)	⑥ nose
⑦ mouth	⑧ tooth (teeth)	⑨ ear(s)	⑩ neck	⑪ shoulder(s)	
⑫ arm(s)	⑬ elbow(s)	⑭ hand(s)	⑮ finger(s)	⑯ stomach	⑰ back
⑱ hip(s)	⑲ leg(s)	⑳ knee(s)	㉑ foot (feet)	㉒ toe(s)	

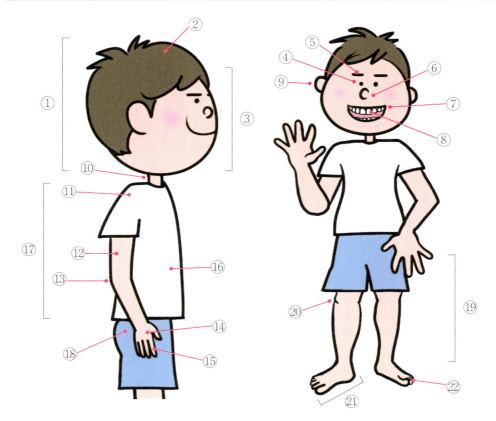

◆ Song: *Head, Shoulders, Knees and Toes* ♪　　🎧 58

歌詞に出てきた体の部位にふれながら歌いましょう。慣れてきたら徐々に速くしていきます。

◆ "Simon Says" Game

体の部位の単語を使い、下線部を変えて "Simon Says" を行ってみましょう。

Simon says, "Touch your _____." / "Shake your _____."

UNIT 9: Activities at a Kindergarten

 Useful Expressions

覚えておきたいフレーズを学びましょう。

◆ **Word Order**

"Duck, Duck, Goose"* は「ハンカチ落とし」に似た、英語圏で人気の遊びです。以下の語を並び替えて、遊び方を完成させましょう。* Dialogue—Substitution Drill も参照。

1. 子どもたちを円状に座らせます。鬼をひとり選びます。

   Have the _____.

   in / circle / sit / a / children

   Choose one person to be "it."

2. 鬼は、円の周りを歩きながら、ひとりずつの頭に軽くふれ "duck" と言います。

   "It" walks around the circle, touching _____

   each / on / head / the / child

   _____ and saying "duck."

3. 鬼が、ある子どもにふれて "goose" と言ったら、その子は立って鬼を追いかけます。

   When "it" touches someone and says "goose," that _____

   _____ "it."

   stands / and / chases / child / up

4. 鬼が（そのままひと回りして）"goose" がいた場所に座れたら、"goose" が次の鬼になります。

   If "it" gets back to where "goose" was sitting and sits down, "goose"

   _____ game.

   next / becomes / the / "it" / for

5. もし "goose" が鬼を捕まえたら、"goose" は座り、鬼はまた鬼にならなければなりません。

   If "goose" tags "it," "goose" sits down, and "it" _____

   _____.

   to / has / again/ "it" / be

小学校外国語教育　知っておきたい基礎知識
（3）さまざまな活動例

　Unit 6〜9 では、ビンゴゲームやミッシング・ゲーム、カードゲーム、"Simon Says" など、さまざまなゲーム的活動が出てきました。文部科学省の教材 "Hi, friends!" 掲載の活動を含め、広く使える、知っておくとよい活動の例を紹介します。

■聞く活動の例
　既習の語彙・表現を復習し、音声に慣れ親しむことが主な目的。習った表現を集中して聞き、反応したり英語で答えたりする活動など。（本書 p. 46 で紹介しているビンゴゲーム、p. 48 のマッチング・カードゲーム、p. 60 の "Simon Says" などは、主に聞く活動となる）

●ポインティング・ゲーム

①語彙・表現の導入に使用した絵カードなどを黒板に貼る。または、関連するテキストのページや既習のものが描かれたワークシートを使ったり、児童用カードを机の上に順不同に並べさせて行ったりすることもできる。

②先生が言う語を聞いて、当てはまる絵や絵カードを児童が指差す。慣れてきたら、複数の単語を先生が言ったあとで、その順序どおりに指を差させる「メモリーゲーム」にすることもできる。

●フルーツ・バスケット（椅子だけを使って行う）
①数字やアルファベット、食べ物やスポーツなどが描かれた、手札サイズの絵カードを、1 枚ずつ、または複数枚児童に持たせる。
②先生が英語を言い、聞こえたもののカードを持っている児童だけが席を移動する。複数の単語を聞かせたり、児童に先生役をさせて発話の練習にしたりすることもできる。「フルーツ・バスケット」と言ったら、全員が移動する。

●ジェスチャー・ゲーム（「気持ち」「スポーツ」「1 日の生活」などに関する内容で）
①例えば、happy / sad（気持ち）、baseball / soccer（スポーツ）、get up / have breakfast（1 日の生活）などの英語表現を、先生がジェスチャーとともに英語を聞かせて導入する。児童はジェスチャーをまねる。
②先生が英語だけを聞かせて、児童はそれに合ったジェスチャーを行う。

③音声に十分に慣れたら、先生がジェスチャーを行い、児童が英語を言う活動にもできる。グループごとに、先生役を交代しながら行い、できるだけたくさんやり取りを行わせる活動にすることもできる。

●スリーヒント・クイズ
　例えば banana が答えであれば、児童が知っている語彙から、fruit / yellow / monkeys など、3 つのヒントを出し、What's this? で尋ねて答えさせる。What's this? を使ったクイズとして、絵カードの一部だけを見せる、シルエットを見せて尋ねる、漢字の読み方をクイズにするなどのさまざまな方法がある。

■話す活動の例

　語彙・表現を十分に聞いて理解できる段階で、実際に使えるようにするために練習を行うことが目的。十分に慣れ親しんだら、実際に英語を使ってコミュニケーションを行う活動へつなげる。（本書 p. 45 で紹介しているミッシング・ゲームは、主に話すことにつなげる練習としての活動となる）

●伝言ゲーム
　①列ごとに、後ろの人に英語を伝言していく。例えば好きな色について、一番前の児童が I like pink. と後ろの児童に伝え、さらに後ろの児童に正確に情報を伝えていく。最後列の児童が当てはまるカードなどを黒板に貼り、正しく情報を伝えられたか確認する。
　②最前列の児童が言った答えに、次の児童が自分の答えを加えて伝え、徐々に情報の量を増やしていく形式もできる。例えば好きな色の伝言ゲームであれば、児童1が pink と児童2に伝え、児童2は、自分の好きな blue を加えて、児童3に pink, blue と伝える、など。

●インタビューゲーム
　①記入用のワークシートを児童に配布する。
　②例えば、Do you like dogs / cats ? Yes, I do. / No, I don't. などの表現を学習したあとで、実際に友達に好き嫌いなどを尋ねる活動を行う。ペアになったり、質問ごとに聞く相手を替えたりして英語でインタビューを行う。聞く前に答えを予想させてから行ってもよい。お互いに知らない情報を、英語を使って交換できるようにすることがポイント。

■発表活動、タスクの例

　習った語彙・表現を用いて、英語を使ってスピーチをしたり、グループで成果物を作って発表したり、英語を使って何らかの目的を達成する活動などの、より発展的な活動。

●ショウ・アンド・テル (show and tell)
　「私の好きなもの」「私の家族」「私の夢」など、習った語彙・表現を用いて、絵や写真、実物などを友達に見せながら紹介する。十分に慣れたらクラス全体で発表会にしてもよい。簡単な表現でも、「言いたいことを英語で伝えられた」という体験が、次の学習への動機づけになる。自己表現活動が、友達についての新しい発見や相互理解にもつながる。

●スキット作り、オリジナルの英語劇作りなど
　学習した内容をもとに、グループなどでオリジナルのスキットや、簡単な英語劇を作って発表する。児童のアイディア、オリジナリティを生かしたクリエイティブな活動となる。

●私の町紹介
　外国の人に、学校や地域を紹介することを目的に、英語の地図をグループで作って発表するような活動。児童にとって達成感が得られ、協同学習の面からも有意義な活動となる（Unit 12 Making a Town Map 参照）。

＊参考資料：成美堂『小学校外国語活動の進め方―「ことばの教育」として―』
　　　　　　文部科学省 WEB サイト

（文責：編集部）

# Growing Plants & Observing the Butterfly Lifecycle

生活科や理科では、朝顔の栽培やチョウの一生について学びます。ALTのケイティも、その内容に関心を持ったようです。他教科に関連する身近な英語表現も学びましょう。

1年生が鉢に何かを植えている様子をケイティが興味深そうに見て、斉藤先生に質問をしています。児童がどんな学習をしているのか考えながら聞きましょう。

◆ **Listen, Fill in & Repeat** 60

会話を聞いて空欄を埋めましょう。意味を確認し、英語を練習しましょう。

Katie: What are the first grade students[1] doing?
Mr. Saito: They're planting morning glory seeds[2].
Katie: Really? They all look (　　　　　).
Mr. Saito: Yes. Each student gets his or her own planter.
Katie: Oh, that's nice.
Mr. Saito: The students are going to take care of (　　　　　) own plants.
Katie: Good for (　　　　　).
Mr. Saito: They'll keep a picture journal (　　　　　) the growth of their plants.
Katie: What a great[3] project!
Mr. Saito: Yes. This is a Life Environmental Studies* project.

*Life Environmental Studies 生活科

◆ Substitution Drill

左のダイアログの下線部に以下の語句を入れ替え、ペアで練習しましょう。

1	the second grade students	the second graders
2	soybeans	sunflower seeds
3	an excellent	a wonderful

🎧 Listening

3年生の理科の授業では、どんな学習をしているのでしょうか。担任の先生は何を持ってきて、子どもたちは何を観察しようとしているのか、気をつけて聞きましょう。

◆ True or False　　　　　　　　　　　　　　　🎧 61

内容と一致するものはT (True)、異なるものはF (False) にチェック ✓ しましょう。

　　　　　　　　　　　　　　　　　　　　　　　　　T 　F

1. The students are learning about trees in their science class. ☐ ☐

2. The homeroom teacher brought in little butterfly eggs on a leaf. ☐ ☐

3. The students brought in leaves for the caterpillars to eat. ☐ ☐

Column　　CLIL（クリル）：内容言語統合型学習

　内容（社会や理科などの教科など）と言語の学習を統合した教授法を CLIL（Content and Language Integrated Learning）と言います。近年、欧州の外国語教育で広く取り入れられ、日本でも注目されています。この教授法を通して、学習者は外国語の四技能（listening、reading、writing、speaking）を高め、考える力、コミュニケーション力を育むことができるとされています。小学校では他教科で学んでいる内容を、英語の授業でも部分的に取り入れるなど、無理のないように CLIL の実践を取り入れていくとよいでしょう。本書では Unit 10-12 において、生活科、理科、家庭科、社会科の内容を英語の授業と結びつける例を紹介しています。

Reading

小学校での朝顔の栽培について書かれています。どんな手順で育て、次の年度の児童のために、何をするのでしょうか。栽培の様子について読みましょう。

◆ Word Match   CD 62

以下の語句の意味を下の日本語から選び、記号を書きましょう。

1. flowerpot ☐　2. soil ☐　3. surface ☐　4. index finger ☐
5. fertilizer ☐　6. vine ☐　7. support stick ☐　8. bud ☐
9. to dry up ☐　10. tradition ☐

| a. つる | b. 土 | c. つぼみ | d. 枯れる | e. 表面 |
| f. 人差し指 | g. 肥料 | h. 支柱 | i. 植木鉢 | j. 恒例の行事 |

CD 63

Growing Morning Glories

Growing morning glories is a hands-on learning experience common to first graders in Japan. Morning glories grow fast, so the project holds students' interest. The students want to show their plants to their friends and teachers and talk about them. This makes the project good for communication, too.

In May, each student receives his or her own large flowerpot. The students put soil in, make the surface flat, and make holes using their index finger. They put one seed in each hole, cover the holes with soil, and water the soil. The pots are placed in a sunny place. When the leaves open, the students put fertilizer in. Vines grow, and students cut some of them. They put in support sticks to help the plants grow tall. When buds appear and the flowers open, students are so happy.

In the summer, students take care of their morning glories at home. They enjoy the flowers, and when the flowers dry up, they pick the seeds. Students bring the seeds back to school in autumn to be saved for the next year's first graders. This tradition continues year after year.

Do you remember growing morning glories when you were in the first grade?

◆ Comprehension Check

左の英文に関する質問の答えを a〜c の中から選びましょう。

1. Why is the project good for communication?
   a. Because the students water their plants.
   b. Because the students want to talk about their plants.
   c. Because the students make holes and plant seeds.

2. What do the students do before they plant the seeds?
   a. They put soil, water, and fertilizer in the pot.
   b. They make holes with their index finger.
   c. They cover the seeds with soil and fertilizer.

3. What do the students bring back to school in the autumn?
   a. They bring back buds and flowers.
   b. They bring back soil and fertilizer.
   c. They bring back seeds for the next year's first graders.

Grammar Point

（　）内の適切な語を選び、日本語に合う英文を完成させましょう。

1. ケイティは（自分が教えている）児童がとても好きです。ほとんどの児童はケイティの英語の授業を楽しんでいます。

   Katie likes (her / his / their) students very much. Most of (her / him / them) enjoy her English lessons.

2. アンディは自分のクラスで何本かのアニメのビデオを使用しました。それらは児童が内容を理解するのに大変役立ちました。

   Andy used some animated videos in (her / his / their) classes. (It / They) helped his students understand the content very well.

［人称代名詞］代名詞は名詞の代わりに使われる語です。人称代名詞は、人称（一人称・二人称・三人称）、格（主格・所有格・目的格）、数（単数・複数）により、形が決まります。代名詞が何を指しているかを理解することが大切です。

Topic 10: Morning Glories

植物の栽培に関わる表現を学びましょう。

◆ Word Match & Song ♪

以下は朝顔の栽培の手順について、簡単な英語で作られた詞です。音声を聞き、空欄に当てはまる語を下から選んで書き、詞を完成させましょう（同じ語を何回か使います）。イラストを見ながら練習した後に、グループで詞に合う動作を考えて発表しましょう。

Morning (①   ), *asagao*,

Pretty flowers, pretty flowers,

Make (②   ), plant the seeds,

Water, (③   ), grow, grow, grow.

Look, look, coming up,

Coming up, coming up,

(④   ), (⑤   ), grow, grow, grow,

(⑥   ), (⑦   ), grow, grow, grow.

I see (⑧   ), I see (⑨   ),

White and pink, purple and blue,

I see brown (⑩   ), pick, pick, pick,

Brown (⑪   ), pick, pick, pick.

（複数回使用します）

a. buds	**b.** flowers	**c.** sunshine	**d.** seeds
e. holes	**f.** vines	**g.** glories	**h.** leaves

UNIT 10: Growing Plants & Observing the Butterfly Lifecycle

Useful Expressions

覚えておきたいフレーズを学びましょう。

Word Order

チョウの一生を表す表現です。イラストに合うように、単語を並び替えて文を完成させましょう。次に、イラストを見ながら言ってみましょう。

Butterfly Lifecycle

1. 小さい卵が葉にくっついています。

    A little egg _____.

    on / leaf / is / a

2. 卵から幼虫が出てきました。

    A caterpillar* _____ egg.

    out / the / of / comes   (*caterpillar 幼虫、青虫)

3. 青虫が葉を食べて、大きくなります。脱皮します。

    The caterpillar _____. It sheds* its skin.

    grows / leaves / eats / and   (*shed 脱皮する)

4. 青虫がさなぎになりました。さなぎの中で、青虫はチョウに変身します。

    The caterpillar makes a pupa*. In the pupa, the caterpillar

    _____.

    butterfly / into / changes / a   (*pupa さなぎ)

5. チョウがさなぎから出てきます。

    The butterfly comes _____.

    of / out / pupa / the

UNIT 11 Making *Onigiri* and Curry

6年生は家庭科で、おにぎりやカレーを作ります。斉藤先生とケイティは、この内容を英語の授業に取り入れてみたいと考えています。

 **Dialogue**

斉藤先生のクラスが、家庭科で調理実習をする話を聞き、ケイティが関心を持ちます。どのように英語の授業に取り入れようとしているのか、考えながら聞きましょう。

◆ **Listen, Fill in & Repeat**　 66

会話を聞いて、空欄を埋めましょう。次に英語をくり返して言いましょう。

Mr. Saito: Our students will make *onigiri*[1] in home economics class.
Katie: That sounds like fun.
Mr. Saito: I'll be helping, too. Do you want to (　　　　　) us?
Katie: Sure. I like *onigiri*[1], but I have never made one (　　　　　).
Mr. Saito: It's not difficult. You can (　　　　　) it easily.
Katie: OK. I'll try.[2]
Mr. Saito: Then you can teach the students how to make *onigiri*[1] using English.
Katie: OK. I'll make a chant to teach how to make *onigiri*[1] in English with actions.
Mr. Saito: Oh, that'll (　　　　　) great!

◆ **Substitution Drill**

左のダイアログの下線部に以下の語句を入れ替え、ペアで練習しましょう。

1	*miso* soup	curry
2	I'll do my best.	I think I can do it.

◆ **Listening**

ケイティは、太郎と紗絵とおにぎりについて話します。3人の好きな具は何か、気をつけて聞きましょう。

◆ **True or False** 67

内容と一致するものはT (True)、異なるものはF (False) にチェック ✓ しましょう。

1. Sae is going to make *onigiri* today.
2. Katie has never tried salmon *onigiri*.
3. Taro's favorite *onigiri* is cod roe *onigiri*.

Column　英語による授業と教室英語

　高等学校や中学校の英語の授業は「英語で行うことを基本とする」方向で進んでおり、先生が英語を使うと同時に、生徒自身が英語を使う機会を増やすことが求められています。小学校でも、まず先生が積極的に英語を使うことが大切です。その手始めに覚えたいのが、授業の進行に使う「教室英語：Classroom English」です。まずは "Good job!" "Nice try!" などのほめ言葉から始めてみましょう（Unit 5 Topic 5 参照）。

　英語の授業では、子どもが理解できる工夫も必要です。ゲームの説明などは、英語で長々と行うより、やって見せるほうが伝わります。言葉だけでなく、デモンストレーション、ジェスチャーのほか、絵カードなどの教材やICTを活用することも理解を助けます。なお、ねらいを伝えたり、振り返りを行ったりする場面では、母語できちんと内容を伝えることも大切と言えるでしょう。

📖 Reading

家庭科の授業で行った調理実習の内容を、英語でも取り入れることになりました。カレーの作り方について読みましょう。

◆ Word Match 🎧 68

以下の語句の意味を下の日本語から選び、記号を書きましょう。

1. procedure ☐
2. cutting board ☐
3. ladle ☐
4. serving ☐
5. to peel ☐
6. to heat ☐
7. to fry ☐
8. to turn down ☐
9. to stir ☐
10. stove ☐

a. 熱する	b. 皮をむく	c. まな板	d. ～人前
e. いためる	f. お玉(杓子)	g. かき回す	h. (調理用)レンジ
i. 手順	j. (火力を)弱める		

🎧 69

Making Curry in Home Economics Class

The students in the sixth grade are making curry next week in their home economics class. Today, they worked in groups and wrote down the things needed to make curry, the ingredients for curry, the cooking procedure, and some important things to remember.

- **Things needed:** cutting boards, kitchen knives, peelers*, pots*, spatulas*, ladles, plates, and spoons. Each student will bring an apron, a bandana, and a dishcloth*.

- **Ingredients for 4 servings:** 2 onions, 1 carrot, 3 potatoes, 250 grams of meat, 1 tablespoon* of oil, 3 1/2 cups of water, curry roux* for 4 servings, salt and pepper.

- **Cooking procedure:** First, wash the potatoes and carrots. Then peel the potatoes, carrots, and onions. Next, cut the vegetables and meat. Heat the oil in the pot. Fry the vegetables and meat, adding salt and pepper. Add water and bring to a boil*. Turn down the heat and cook until the vegetables are soft. Add the curry roux, stir, and cook for twenty minutes.

- **Important things to remember:** Use the kitchen knife and stove safely, clean up well, and cooperate as a group.

*peeler 皮むき　*pot なべ　*spatula フライ返し　*dishcloth ふきん　*tablespoon 大さじ
*roux (煮込み料理の)ルー (元はフランス語)　*bring to a boil 沸騰させる

◆ Comprehension Check

左の英文に関する質問の答えを a 〜 c の中から選びましょう。

1. What ingredients do the students need to make curry?
   a. They need cutting boards, kitchen knives, and peelers.
   b. They need an apron, a bandana, and a dishcloth.
   c. They need potatoes, onions, carrots, and meat.

2. What should the students do after they fry the vegetables and meat?
   a. They should add curry roux and stir.
   b. They should add water and bring it to a boil.
   c. They should wash and peel the potatoes and carrots.

3. What is important for the students to keep in mind?
   a. They should use the stove safely.
   b. They should sharpen the kitchen knives.
   c. They should work independently.

Grammar Point

（　　）内の適切な語を選び、日本語に合う英文を完成させましょう。

1. 私は、卵、ソーセージ、パン、コーヒーの朝食をとりました。
   I had (a / an / two) egg, (a / an / two) sausages, (a / an / a slice of) toast, and (a cup of / a piece of) coffee for breakfast.

2. ケイティは毎朝、シリアルとバナナを食べます。
   Katie has (a jar of / a bowl of) cereal and (a / an / two) banana every morning.

[名詞] 名詞には、可算名詞（数えられる名詞）と不可算名詞（数えられない名詞）があります。可算名詞は、単数の場合は a / an がついたり、複数の場合は -(e)s などがつきます。不可算名詞の場合、複数形にはなりませんが、a 〜 of ... / two 〜 s of ... などで数を表すことができます。

Topic 11: Let's Make *Onigiri*!

おにぎりの作り方を簡単な英語で学びましょう。

◆ Sentence Match & Chant   CD 70

イラストに合う英語を下から選び、記号を入れましょう。次にチャンツを聞いて言ってみます。言えるようになったら、動作をつけてみましょう。（6と9は同じ表現です。）

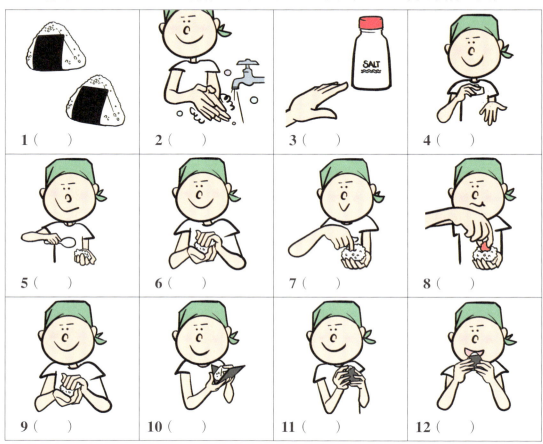

1 (　)　2 (　)　3 (　)　4 (　)
5 (　)　6 (　)　7 (　)　8 (　)
9 (　)　10 (　)　11 (　)　12 (　)

- **a.** Let's make rice balls!
- **b.** *Umeboshi* in.
- **c.** Rice in.
- **d.** Wash your hands.
- **e.** Make a hole.
- **f.** Shape, shape.
- **g.** Shake, shake.
- **h.** Salt, salt.
- **i.** Eat it! Eat it!
- **j.** *Nori* on.
- **k.** Wrap it, wrap it.

◆ Practice

Umeboshi（pickled plum）を以下のような他の具にして、同様に言ってみましょう。

　　shake (salmon), *tarako* (cod roe), *okaka* (bonito flakes), *konbu* (kelp), etc.

UNIT 11: Making *Onigiri* and Curry

Useful Expressions

覚えておきたいフレーズを学びましょう。

◆ Word Order

カレーの作り方です。単語を並び替えて文を完成させましょう。

1. 野菜を洗って、皮をむきましょう。

   Wash _____.

   and / vegetables / the / peel

2. 野菜と肉を切りましょう。塩・こしょうを加えながらいためます。

   Cut the vegetables and meat.

   Fry _____ pepper.

   and / adding / them / salt

3. 水を加えて、すべて煮ます。

   Add _____.

   and / everything / cook / water

4. カレールーを加えて20分煮ます。

   Put curry roux in and _____.

   minutes / cook / for / twenty

5. カレーをごはんと一緒に食べましょう。

   Eat _____.

   curry / rice / the / with

peel

cut

fry

cook

UNIT 12 Making a Town Map

外国語（英語）担当の斉藤先生とケイティは、社会科の学習内容を英語の授業に生かせないか相談しています。どんな内容をどのように取り入れるのでしょうか。

 Dialogue

児童は地域の地図作りをしてうれしそうです。ケイティがどのような着想を得たのか、考えながら聞きましょう。

◆ **Listen, Fill in & Repeat**   72

会話を聞いて空欄（各2語）を埋めましょう。意味を確認し、英語を練習しましょう。

> Katie: The students looked so excited. <u>Where did they go?</u>[1]
> Mr. Saito: They (　　　　　　　　　　) to draw a map of this town.
> Katie: Really?
> Mr. Saito: Each student got a (　　　　　　　　　　) only the main streets and the river. Then the students added <u>other places</u>[2] on the maps.
> Katie: Oh, (　　　　　　　　　　).
> Mr. Saito: Can you combine this study with your English lesson?
> Katie: Yes. How about having the students make English town maps for foreign guests?
> Mr. Saito: That sounds good.
> Katie: I can teach <u>easy instructions</u>[3] for making a map and the names of places.

UNIT 12: Making a Town Map

◆ Substitution Drill

左のダイアログの下線部に以下の語句を入れ替え、ペアで練習しましょう。

1	What did they do?	What happened?
2	public places	historical places
3	useful expressions	English phrases

Listening

ケイティは授業でどのような点に注意して教えているのか、気をつけて聞きましょう。

◆ True or False

 73

内容と一致するものはT (True)、異なるものはF (False) にチェック ✓ しましょう。

　　　　　　　　　　　　　　　　　　　　　　　　　　　　　T　F

1. The students will repeat what Katie says in English. ☐ ☐

2. The students have trouble saying "convenience store." ☐ ☐

3. The students will work in groups of three or four. ☐ ☐

Column　外来語の活用

　子どもたちの回りには、外来語（カタカナ英語）があふれています。本ユニットで出てくる建物の名前のほかに、国名（オーストラリア等）、動物（ペンギン等）、食べ物（ハンバーガー等）、本来とは異なる音声で定着したものがたくさんあります。これらを「英語学習の邪魔」とする声もありますが、上手に活用する方法もあります。例えば英語だけを聞かせ「みんながよく知っている言葉だけど何だろう？」と考えさせたり、日本語と英語を聞かせ「どこが違うかな？」と比較させたりすれば、英語の特徴、日本語との違いへの気づきを促す活動になります。国語の時間に習うローマ字についても同様で、英語の文字と関連づけて指導することも考えられます。既に知っている多数の語や知識を上手に利用して、英語学習に役立たせられるとよいでしょう。

Reading

担任の先生とケイティは児童が授業で作業を行っている様子を見たり、手伝ったりしています。児童はどんな作業をしているのか、読みましょう。

◆ Word Match CD 74

以下の語句の意味を下の日本語から選び、記号を書きましょう。

1. to integrate ☐ 2. social studies ☐ 3. to explore ☐
4. detail ☐ 5. neatly ☐ 6. to label ☐ 7. police station ☐
8. fire station ☐ 9. opposite ~ ☐ 10. finishing touch ☐

| a. 仕上げ | b. ～の反対に | c. 詳細 | d. 消防署 | e. 警察署 |
| f. きちんと・きれいに | g. 社会科 | h. 表示する | i. 探検する | j. 統合する |

CD 75

Making English Town Maps

Katie is working with the homeroom teacher to integrate social studies with English. First, the students explored their town and filled in places on a map with some information in Japanese. Now they are working in groups to make large English town maps. They are drawing and coloring pictures of places and pasting the English place names on their maps. Katie stops to admire Group A's work. Their map is colorful, full of details, and neatly labeled. It shows the police station, city hall, fire station, hospital, and supermarket on Chuo Street. The map is nearly finished. One girl is placing a flower shop next to the hospital. Another girl is gluing a department store opposite the police station. A boy is placing the library between the police station and the city hall. Another boy is placing a convenience store in front of the hospital. Other students are working on finishing touches. They are working together well.

As the students work, they comment on the many good points of their town and the places they would like to show foreign guests. In the next lesson, the students will try introducing their town in simple English using their maps.

UNIT 12: Making a Town Map

◆ Comprehension Check

左の英文に関する質問の答えを a 〜 c の中から選びましょう。

1. What are the students working on?
   a. They are working on their science project.
   b. They are working on a map of their town.
   c. They are working on their homework.

2. Why does Katie admire Group A's work?
   a. Because the students are speaking and moving around.
   b. Because there is a flower shop next to the hospital.
   c. Because their map is colorful and neatly labeled.

3. What will the students do in the next lesson?
   a. They will make a large English map of their town.
   b. They will try introducing their town using simple English.
   c. They will walk through the town and fill in places on a map.

Grammar Point

（　）内の適切な語句を選び、英文を完成させましょう。

1. 郵便局は並木通りに面しています。通りをはさんで博物館の向かいにあります。
   The post office is (in / on / at) Namiki Street. It's (behind / opposite / by) the museum.

2. 靴屋はサクラ通りとツツジ通りの間にあります。
   The shoe store is (next to / between / among) Sakura Street and Tsutsuji Street.

[場所を表す前置詞] 前置詞は基本的に（代）名詞の前に置かれます。場所を表す前置詞には、**on**（〈通り〉に面して）、**opposite / across from**（〈通りをはさんで〉反対に）、**between A and B**（AとBの間に）、**next to** 〜（〜の隣に）、**in front of** 〜（〜の前に）、**behind**（後ろに）、**by** 〜（〜のそばに）などがあります。

81

🏢 Topic 12: Town Map

いろいろな場所の名称について学びましょう。

◆ Practice & Chant 🎧 76

地図を見て場所の言い方を確認しましょう。次に音声を聞いて練習しましょう。

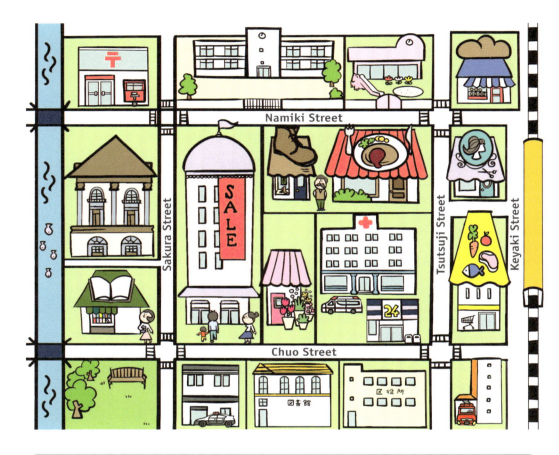

① post office　② elementary school　③ kindergarten　④ bakery
⑤ station　⑥ museum　⑦ department store　⑧ shoe store
⑨ restaurant　⑩ hairdresser's　⑪ bookstore　⑫ flower shop
⑬ hospital　⑭ convenience store　⑮ supermarket　⑯ park
⑰ police station　⑱ library　⑲ city hall　⑳ fire station

◆ More Practice

上の地図をもとに、場所についての聞き方と答え方を練習しましょう。

Q: Where is the …?
A: It's [on … street / across from … / between … and … / next to …].

UNIT 12: Making a Town Map

👉 Useful Expressions

覚えておきたいフレーズを学びましょう。

◆ Word Order

工作に関する表現です。単語を並び替えて文を完成させましょう。

1. グループの人と協力して、作業をしましょう。

    Work together with _____.

    of / the / your / members / group

2. 町の絵を鉛筆で描いて下さい。

    Draw a _____ using a pencil.

    of / town / our / picture

3. マーカー（マジック）で絵に色をぬりなさい。

    Color _____.

    markers / using / picture / the

4. 画用紙に英語を写しましょう。

    Copy the English words _____.

    the / paper / construction / on

5. 絵を切り抜いて、地図に貼りましょう。

    Cut out the pictures _____ the map.

    on / them / and / paste*

    *"glue"（のりで貼る）や"tape"（テープで貼る）も使えます。

◆ School Supplies

工作に必要な文具等の言い方も学びましょう。

You will need your _____.

scissors   colored pencils   glue   markers   tape   stapler

小学校でのCLILの実践例（実際の授業の様子より）

　本書のUnit10-12では、他教科の学習内容を英語に取り入れるCLIL（内容言語統合型学習）を紹介しました（p. 67 Column参照）。外国語学習の時間に教科内容を部分的に英語で学ぶ形であれば、日本の小学校でもCLILを無理なく導入できる可能性があります。筆者らが教えている小学校で行っている、CLILの実践*を一部ご紹介します。3年生の理科で学習する「チョウの一生」を題材とした英語の授業の様子です。

■教師と児童との英語でのやり取り～チョウ・昆虫について～

　教師が児童に、理科の教科書の「昆虫・チョウのそだちかた」の写真と絵をプロジェクタで見せます。教師（T）と児童（Ss）のやり取りを見てみましょう。英語でのやり取りを通して、違った角度から同じトピックを学ぶことができ、理解が深まるとともに、新たな発見も生まれます。
　以下は、モンシロチョウの卵や青虫についてのやり取りです。

●モンシロチョウについての会話

T:	What's this?	（これは何ですか。）
Ss:	It's an egg.	（卵です。）
T:	Yes. What color is it?	（そうですね。何色ですか。）
Ss:	It's yellow.	（黄色。）
T:	Yes, it's light yellow. Is the egg round or oval?	（はい。薄い黄色ですね。卵は丸ですか、楕円ですか。）
Ss:	It's oval.	（楕円。）
T:	Yes. Look at this caterpillar. What is it eating?	（そうです。この青虫を見てください。何を食べていますか。）
Ss:	Cabbage.	（キャベツ。）
T:	Yes. *Monshirocho* is "cabbage butterfly" in English.	（はい。モンシロチョウは英語で「キャベッジ・バタフライ」と言います。）
Ss:	Really?	（えー。本当ですか。）

　次は昆虫の体とつくりについてのやり取りです。生き物を分析的に観察し、足の数と体の部位を根拠として、昆虫とそれ以外の生き物を区別する学習が英語で行われています。

●昆虫についての会話

T:	*Konchu* is "insect" in English.	（昆虫は英語で「インセクト」と言います。）
T:	Is a butterfly an insect?	（バタフライはインセクトですか。）
Ss:	Yes.	（はい。）
T:	How many legs do you see?	（足は何本ありますか。）
Ss:	Six.	（6本。）
T:	Yes. Insects have six legs. Look at the butterfly. How many body parts do you see?	（そうです。昆虫の足は6本です。チョウを見てください。体はいくつに分かれていますか。）
Ss:	Three.	（3つです。）
T:	Yes. Insects have three body parts.	（そうですね。昆虫の体は3つに分かれています。）

T: Is a spider an insect?	（クモは昆虫ですか。）
Ss: Umm…	（えーと…）
T: Can you count the legs?	（足の数を数えてみてください。）
Ss: One, two, three, … eight.	（1、2、3、…8。）
T: Yes, eight legs.	（そうですね。8本です。
So, a spider is not an insect.	ですから、クモは昆虫ではありませんね。）

■表現の導入から定着、グループ発表まで～動作や歌を通して～

　チョウの成長過程についての英語表現は、動作を活用したTPRの指導法（p.59 Column参照）で導入します。まず教師が、表現に合った動作をしながら英語を児童に聞かせます。次に児童が、英語を聞いて動作で反応します。さらに、チョウ（メス）の一生を歌にした*Butterfly Lifecycle Song*を「ちょうちょ」の替え歌で動作とともに歌い、表現の定着を図ります。最後に、グループごとに、チョウの一生を歌や劇で表現する練習をし、みんなの前で発表します。劇の場合、セリフは歌詞と同じものです。

　児童は、脱皮の様子を表すために、Tシャツの中に頭を入れてその中から出てきたり、糸を出してさなぎが枝や葉につく様子を、体をくるくる回して表現したりと、独創的なアイディアを見せてくれます。

●*Butterfly Lifecycle Song* ♪　　チョウの一生の歌　　※カッコ内は英語に合わせて行う動作を示す

Little egg on a leaf	（小さい卵が葉についている。）
Caterpillar come on out	（幼虫が卵から出てくる。）
Eat, eat, eat, grow, grow, grow	（たくさん食べて、成長する。）
Shed your skin, and grow	（脱皮して、また、大きくなる。）
Make a house, pupa house	（さなぎの家を作る。）
Change, change, come on out	（変身して、出てくる。）
Butterfly, fly, fly, fly	（チョウが飛ぶ。）
Lay your eggs and fly away	（卵を産んで飛び去って行く。）

　さなぎがチョウになる場面では、児童は"Come on out! Butterfly, fly, fly, fly!"と言って盛り上がります。CLILの授業の後では「理科もこうやるとおもしろいね」「次はトンボやカエルの一生もやってほしい」という声も聞かれます。みんなで協力して、楽しみながら覚えた英語と学習内容は、しっかりと身につくようです。

　このような実践を踏まえ、児童はCLILを通じて、自分の英語に自信を持ち、これからの英語学習へのモチベーションを高められる可能性があると考えています。

「チョウの一生」について、オリジナルの英語の絵本作り。理科の教科書を参考に、挿絵を描く。

＊聖学院小学校（東京）での実践より。同校では教科として全学年、週2コマ、英語を教えている。専門の英語講師と外国人講師が、単独でまたはティーム・ティーチングで授業を行う。英語のカリキュラムや教材は、CLILを取り入れたものも含め、独自のものを多く使用。筆者らは同様な取り組みを公立小学校でも行っている。

UNIT 13 Introducing Japanese Culture

国際交流のために来日したオーストラリアの小学生が、南小学校を訪れます。児童は日本の文化や習慣を英語で紹介することになりました。

 Dialogue

オーストラリアの小学生との交流予定について戸田先生とアンディが話しています。内容を考えながら聞きましょう。

◆ **Listen, Fill in & Repeat**　CD 78

会話を聞いて空欄（各2語）を埋めましょう。意味を確認し、英語を練習しましょう。

> Ms. Toda: Some students from Australia[1] are visiting our school.
> Andy: Oh, really? What's the purpose of (　　　　　　　)?
> Ms. Toda: Our city has an exchange program with their city in Australia[1].
> Andy: I see. When are they coming (　　　　　　　) school?
> Ms. Toda: On September 30th. Our students are planning to show them origami[2].
> Andy: Great. How (　　　　　　　) help?
> Ms. Toda: Could you teach simple English instructions for how to make origami[3]?
> Andy: Sure. I'll do that in my next class.

UNIT 13: Introducing Japanese Culture

◆ Substitution Drill

左のダイアログの下線部に、以下の語句を入れ替え、練習しましょう。

1	Canada	Germany
2	calligraphy*	*kendama*
3	write calligraphy	play *kendama*

＊書道・書写

 Listening

南小学校の児童は、オーストラリアの小学生に、折り紙の作り方を紹介します。何を作り、どのような遊びを紹介するのか、気をつけて聞きましょう。

◆ True or False 79

内容と一致するものはT (True)、異なるものはF (False) にチェック ✓ しましょう。

　　　　　　　　　　　　　　　　　　　　　　　　　　　　　　　　T　F

1. The Japanese student taught origami to the Australian student. ☐ ☐

2. It was too difficult for the Australian student to make a frog. ☐ ☐

3. The Australian student won the frog race. ☐ ☐

> **Column**　日本文化の発信
>
> 　外国からのゲストに、自分たちのこと、また日本の文化・習慣・遊びなどを英語で伝えることは、児童にとって大きな喜びとなります。伝える内容が身近なので、簡単な英語であれば、彼らは自信を持ってコミュニケーションを図ろうとします。英語で伝えることができた喜びは、英語学習のさらなる動機づけになるとともに、自国の文化に対する認識を高めることにもなります。また、児童が普段から接しているALTに、好きな遊びや場所などを紹介する活動を取り入れ、単元最後の目標にすれば、目的意識を持った学習になります。年間計画を考える際に、外国の方々との交流予定があれば、児童が他教科で学習した日本の事柄などから題材を選び、英語で伝えるための準備をする時間を事前に設けるとよいでしょう。このことは、日本文化を発信する活動にもつながります。

Reading

折り紙は日本の子どもたちが小さい時から慣れ親しんでいるものです。南幼稚園ではどのように折り紙を飾るのか、また、折り紙の教育的利点についても読みましょう。

◆ Word Match　CD 80

以下の語句の意味を下の日本語から選び、記号を書きましょう。

1. crane ☐　2. get-well ☐　3. to display ☐　4. demon ☐
5. benefit ☐　6. to improve ☐　7. concentration ☐
8. to increase ☐　9. creativity ☐　10. to develop ☐

| a. 向上させる | b. 増す | c. 展示する | d. 見舞いの | e. 鶴 |
| f. 恩恵・利点 | g. 創造力 | h. 鬼 | i. 発展させる | j. 集中 |

CD 81

Origami

　Origami is the traditional Japanese art of paper folding. By folding a single piece of square paper, you can make an animal, a toy, a flower, or many other things. Children can play with some of the origami which they make. They play catch with origami balloons and have races with origami frogs. Children also like to give friends origami which they have made. A class sometimes makes origami cranes, which are given to a classmate who is sick for a get-well gift.

　Children who go to Minami Kindergarten make different origami for each season. Their work is then displayed in the classrooms. In spring, they make dolls for the Dolls Festival*, in summer, they make stars for the Star Festival*, in fall, they make chestnuts* and mushrooms, and in winter, they make demons for *Setsubun*.

　Origami is said to have many educational benefits: it improves concentration, increases thinking ability and creativity, and develops motor skills*. Also, when children make origami with their classmates, they have fun together.

　Origami is popular outside of Japan, too. Children in elementary schools around the world enjoy the magic of paper folding.

*the Dolls Festival ひな祭り　*the Star Festival 七夕　*chestnut 栗
*motor skill（折り紙の場合）指先を動かすことにより、大脳の発達を促すこと

UNIT 13: Introducing Japanese Culture

◆ **Comprehension Check**

左の英文に関する質問の答えを a～c の中から選びましょう。

1. How do children play with origami?
   a. They play hide and seek with origami frogs.
   b. They make origami cranes and have a race.
   c. They play catch with origami balloons.

2. What is displayed in Minami Kindergarten in spring?
   a. Origami chestnuts and mushrooms that children make.
   b. Origami dolls that children make for the Dolls Festival.
   c. Origami stars that children make for the Star Festival.

3. What is one of the educational benefits of origami?
   a. It teaches children to have good manners in class.
   b. It helps children to increase their concentration.
   c. It helps children to play outside with friends.

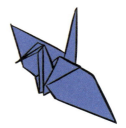

Grammar Point

（　）内の適切な語句を選び、日本語に合う英文を完成させましょう。

1. 日本の幼稚園に通う子どもたちは、折り紙を楽しんでいます。
   Children (which / who / whom) go to a Japanese kindergarten enjoy origami.

2. 子どもたちは、自分で作った折り紙のカエルで遊びます。
   Children play with origami frogs (which / who / whom) they made.

［関係代名詞］接続詞と代名詞の働きを持ち、2文を1文に結合する働きをします。関係代名詞の前には、先行詞が置かれます。先行詞が人か物かにより関係代名詞が異なります。また、関係代名詞には3つの格（主格・所有格・目的格）があり、後に続く節の中での役割によって格は決まります（以下参照）。
- 先行詞（人）：who*（主格）、whose（所有格）、whom*（目的格）
- 先行詞（物）：which*（主格）、whose（所有格）、which*（目的格）

*のついた関係代名詞は that で表すこともできます。

Topic 13: Making Origami

折り紙の作り方を学びましょう。

◆ Read & Practice 　CD 82

イラストを見ながら英文を読み、かぶとの折り方を確認しましょう。次に音声を聞いて練習しましょう。最後に、英語で説明しながら、かぶとを折ってみましょう。

Let's make a *kabuto*, a samurai helmet. Watch and do what I do.

1. White side up.
   Fold it in half and make a triangle.

2. Fold both sides down and make a square.

3. Fold both sides up.

4. Fold it like this and make a small triangle. Do the same on the other side.

5. Fold this up halfway.

6. Fold this up, along the center line.

7. Open. Fold this in.

8. You made a *kabuto*.

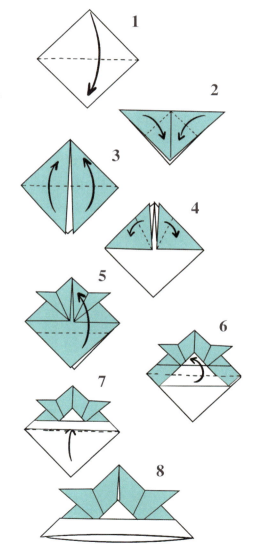

Notes: fold ～ in half ～を半分に折る　fold ～ up / down ～を折り上げる／下げる
　　　 fold ～ like this ～をこのように折る　fold ～ in ～を折り入れる
　　　 do the same 同様にする

UNIT 13: Introducing Japanese Culture

 Useful Expressions

覚えておきたいフレーズを学びましょう。

◆ Word Order

日本の行事についての説明です。下線の日本語に合うように、単語を並び替えて文を完成させましょう。

1. ［元旦　New Year's Day: January 1st］
多くの人が神社や寺に初詣に出かけ、幸せと健康を祈ります。雑煮という<u>伝統的な餅のスープ</u>を食べます。

    Many people visit shrines and temples to pray for happiness and good health. We eat *zoni*, a _____.

    cake / traditional / with / rice / soup

2. ［節分　Bean Throwing Ceremony: February 3rd］
「鬼は外」と言いながら家の外に豆をまいて悪運を追い払い、「福は内」と言いながら家の中に豆をまき<u>幸運を招き入れます</u>。

    We throw beans outside the house while saying, "*oniwasoto*," to drive bad luck away, and throw beans inside, saying "*fukuwauchi*," _____.

    luck / to / in / invite / good

3. ［子どもの日　Children's Day: May 5th］
<u>かぶとを家の中に</u>飾り、鯉のぼりを外に掲げ、子どもが健康で強く成長することを願います。

    We display a *kabuto*, a _____, _____

    helmet / in / samurai / house / the

    and put up *koinobori*, carp streamers, outside and pray for children to stay healthy and grow strong.

4. ［七夕　Star Festival: July 7th］
願いごとを<u>短冊</u>に書いて、笹竹の枝につるします。

    We write our wishes on *tanzaku*, _____,

    strips / paper / colorful / of

    and hang them on branches of a bamboo tree.

UNIT 14 Evacuation Drills

南小学校では毎月、避難訓練を行います。今月は火災訓練があり、ケイティは初めて日本の避難訓練を体験します。避難訓練に関わる表現を学びましょう。

 Dialogue

斉藤先生とケイティが火災訓練について話しています。内容を考えながら聞きましょう。

◆ **Listen, Fill in & Repeat**   84

会話を聞いて空欄を埋めましょう。意味を確認し、英語を練習しましょう。

Mr. Saito: Today, we'll have a fire drill.
Katie: What time (   ) it be?
Mr. Saito: Around 10:20, (   ) the second period.
Katie: OK. What will happen?
Mr. Saito: When we hear the announcement[1], the students will line up in the hall[2] and leave the building quickly.
Katie: Where (   ) we go?
Mr. Saito: We'll go to the playground[3].
Katie: OK. Can I help with anything?
Mr. Saito: Please help the homeroom teacher.
Katie: All right. I'll (   ) my best.

UNIT 14: Evacuation Drills

◆ Substitution Drill

左のダイアログの下線部に、以下の語句を入れ替え、ペアで練習しましょう。

1	see smoke	hear the alarm
2	cover their mouths and crawl on the floor	listen carefully to the announcement
3	near the main gate	to the park next to school

 Listening

消火器の使い方についての説明です。使う順番に気をつけて聞いてみましょう。

◆ True or False

CD 85

内容と一致するものはT (True)、異なるものはF (False) にチェック ✓ しましょう。

              T F

1. Most people know how to use a fire extinguisher.

2. The word PASS stands for Pull, Aim, Stop, and Sweep.

3. The PASS method is important when you use a fire extinguisher.

  Pull   Aim   Squeeze   Sweep

Column　避難訓練

　日本の小学校でも、火災訓練だけでなく、地震があったときの対処などを定めているところが多いようです。非常時の対応については、ALTにも説明しておくことが望ましいでしょう。米国の小学校の避難訓練では、例えば、洋服に火が燃え移ったらどのようにして自分で火を消すか、火災で避難するときにはどのようなことに注意してドアを開けるかなど、小学生でも、自ら危機に対処するための訓練を行っています（Useful Expressions 参照）。

南小学校の避難訓練ではどのようなことをするのでしょうか。非常事態の際、あわてないようにするための標語についても読みましょう。

◆ Word Match

以下の語句の意味を下の日本語から選び、記号を書きましょう。

1. evacuation ☐   2. drill ☐   3. familiar with ～ ☐
4. route ☐   5. injury ☐   6. loss of life ☐   7. to prevent ☐
8. earthquake ☐   9. safety ☐   10. slogan ☐

a. 地震	**b.** 標語	**c.** けが	**d.** 避難	**e.** 安全性	**f.** 訓練
g. （避難）経路	**h.** （物・事柄）に精通している		**i.** 妨げる	**j.** 生命の損失	

Evacuation Drills

Minami Elementary School has a disaster drill once a month. The drills make students familiar with what to do in a disaster.

When the school has a fire drill, the students must know which route to take to get out of the building. If students can learn to get out of the building quickly, injury or loss of life can be prevented in case of an actual fire.

When the school has an earthquake drill, the students get under the desks and wait for an announcement informing everyone of what to do.

Firefighters sometimes come to observe the drills and give a talk about fire safety. They may give students the opportunity to use a fire extinguisher, or come with an earthquake simulation vehicle* in which students can experience a strong earthquake.

Schools in Japan often teach students the slogan, "O-KA-SHI-MO*." O stands for *osanai*, no pushing; KA stands for *kakenai*, no running; SHI stands for *shaberanai*, no talking; and MO stands for *modoranai*, no going back. This slogan helps students remember how to act in an actual disaster.

*earthquake simulation vehicle 起震車　*OHASHIMO も使われる。(HA= 走らない。no running)

| O | – | KA | – | SHI | – | MO |

◆ **Comprehension Check**

左の英文に関する質問の答えを a 〜 c の中から選びましょう。

1. Why are evacuation drills important for students?
   a. Because they make students familiar with what to do in a disaster.
   b. Because they make students worried about disasters.
   c. Because they make students run when they leave the building.

2. What can students experience in the earthquake simulation vehicles?
   a. They can experience getting out of a building quickly.
   b. They can experience a strong earthquake.
   c. They can experience an actual fire.

3. What does O-KA-SHI-MO mean?
   a. It means no pushing, no fighting, no talking, and no looking.
   b. It means no pushing, no running, no sitting, and no going back.
   c. It means no pushing, no running, no talking, and no going back.

Grammar Point

（　）内の適切な語句を選び、日本語に合う英文を完成させましょう。

1. もし大きな地震がきたら、どうしましょうか。
   What shall we do (if / because) a big earthquake occurs?

2. 火災のとき、標語「お・か・し・も」を思い出しなさい。
   (When / Although) there is a fire, remember the slogan, "O-KA-SHI-MO."

［副詞節］主に動詞や主節全体を修飾する節で、時・理由・条件・譲歩などを表わす接続詞、when（〜のとき）、because（〜なので）、if（もし〜なら）、though/although（〜にもかかわらず）を伴います。

Topic 14: Fire Drills

火災訓練に関わる英語の表現を学びましょう。

◆ Sentence Match & Practice

イラストに合う英語を下から選び、記号を書きましょう。次に音声を聞いて練習しましょう。

a. Put your protective head covering on.
b. Listen to the announcement carefully.
c. Don't push other people.
d. Cover your mouth and nose with a wet towel.
e. Stay calm and leave the building quickly.

UNIT 14: Evacuation Drills

👉 Useful Expressions

覚えておきたいフレーズを学びましょう。

◆ Word Order

ケイティが小学生のときに学んだ、火事の際に知っておくとよい知識です。単語を並び替えて文を完成させましょう。

1. もし洋服に火がついたら、立ち止まり、体を低くして、ころがりなさい。

   If _____ ,

   clothes / on / your / are / fire

   you should stop, drop, and roll.

   stop　　　　　　　drop　　　　　　　roll

2. ドアから煙が出ているのを見たら、ドアを開けてはいけません。

   If you _____

   from / smoke / see / coming

   the door, don't open it.

3. ドアが熱いかどうか確かめるには、ドアに手の甲でふれなさい。

   To check if the door is hot, touch the door with

   _____.

   your / of / hand / back / the

4. ドアが熱かったら、ドアを開けてはいません。反対側が火事かもしれません。

   If the door is hot, don't open it because

   _____ on the other side.

   fire / may / there / be

97

UNIT 15 Graduation

3月は6年生の児童とお別れの時期です。学校ではどんなことがあるのでしょうか。また卒業式ではどんなことをするのでしょうか。南小学校の様子を見てみましょう。

 Dialogue

斉藤先生とケイティがお別れ会について話しています。内容を考えながら聞きましょう。

◆ **Listen, Fill in & Repeat**   90

会話を聞いて空欄（各2語）を埋めましょう。意味を確認し、英語を練習しましょう。

> Mr. Saito: Here is the information about a sending-off party for the sixth graders*.
> Katie: What (　　　　　　　　) at the party?
> Mr. Saito: Lots of fun things. <u>Grade four is preparing some games to play with all the grades.</u>¹
> Katie: How nice!
> Mr. Saito: Grade five is going to perform a play in English.
> Katie: What (　　　　　　　　) going to perform?
> Mr. Saito: A <u>popular</u>² Japanese children's story. Andy is helping the students to practice.
> Katie: I (　　　　　　　　) to see it!
> Mr. Saito: The sixth graders are going to sing a song and give a thank-you message to everyone.

*sending-off party for the sixth graders　6年生を送る会。farewell party でもよい。

◆ Substitution Drill

左のダイアログの下線部に、以下の語句を入れ替え、ペアで練習をしましょう。

1	Grades one and two are going to sing and dance.	Grade three is going to play musical instruments.
2	traditional	well-known

🎧 Listening

卒業する児童は、どのように感謝の気持ちを表すのか、気をつけて聞きましょう。

◆ True or False CD 91

内容と一致するものは T (True)、異なるものは F (False) にチェック しましょう。

		T	F
1.	Katie wanted to write thank-you messages to her students.	☐	☐
2.	Mr. Saito translated the students' messages into Japanese.	☐	☐
3.	The students are copying their messages on flower-shaped paper.	☐	☐

Column　国・地域により異なる卒業シーズン

　日本の学校では、4月に入学し、3月に卒業となりますが、国や地域によってそれらの時期は異なります。オーストラリアでは、1月末から2月の初めに学年が始まり12月の初めに終了します。フィリピン共和国では6月に始まり3月に終了します。米国では、9月に始まり5月に終わるので、3カ月近い夏休みがあります。JETプログラムで来日するALTの多くは、大学を卒業したばかりの若者です。彼らは夏休みに来日してオリエンテーションを受け、2学期から学校に勤務します。日本の習慣や学校生活に慣れるには時間がかかりますが、英語を教えることが好きになり、日本に残る人もいます。子どもたちにも良い思い出がたくさんできるよう、ALTとの良好な関係を築きたいものです。

 Reading

日本の小学校の卒業式の様子はどのようなものでしょうか。学校により多少異なりますが、多くの共通点があります。参加者や卒業式の様子について読みましょう。

◆ Word Match 🎧 92

以下の語句の意味を下の日本語から選び、記号を書きましょう。

1. graduation ceremony ☐   2. ritual ☐   3. diploma ☐
4. president ☐   5. applauded ☐   6. sadness ☐   7. to part with ~ ☐
8. appreciation ☐   9. growth ☐   10. impressive ☐

| a. 拍手されて | b. 儀式 | c. 感謝 | d. 悲しみ | e. 卒業式 |
| f. 卒業証書 | g. ～と別れる | h. 会長 | i. 印象的な | j. 成長 |

🎧 93

Graduation at Japanese Elementary Schools

The Japanese school year starts in April and ends in March. A graduation ceremony is held in March. This ritual is an important step for students as they move on in life.

Ceremonies may vary from school to school, but they often include the following. The graduating students enter together and the ceremony begins. The students are called by name, stand up, and go up to the stage one by one to receive their diplomas. The principal, the PTA president, and other guests of honor* offer words of congratulation to the graduates. The graduating students give a choral* farewell message, and the remaining students then respond with a choral message. At the end of the ceremony, the graduates line up and walk out, applauded by all in attendance.

Some students, teachers, and parents, moved by various emotions, may cry during the ceremony. Students may cry tears of sadness at parting with friends and leaving the school where they spent so much time for six years. Parents may cry in appreciation for their child's growth. A Japanese graduation ceremony can be an impressive and memorable experience.

*guests of honor 来賓   *choral 声を合わせた

UNIT 15: Graduation

◆ **Comprehension Check**

左の英文に関する質問の答えを a ～ c の中から選びましょう。

1. What do graduation ceremonies typically include?
    a. Speeches by ALTs.
    b. The presentation of diplomas.
    c. Graduation lunch under the cherry blossoms.

2. How do the students receive their diplomas?
    a. They receive their diplomas one by one on the stage.
    b. They receive their diplomas from the PTA president.
    c. They receive their diplomas one by one from their parents.

3. What are Japanese graduation ceremonies like?
    a. They are impressive.
    b. They are discouraging.
    c. They are forgettable.

Grammar Point

(　　) 内の適切な語句を選び、日本語に合う英文を完成させましょう。

1. 児童はハートの形をした紙にメッセージを書きました。
    Students wrote their messages on heart-(shaping / shaped) paper.

2. 親は子どもたちが卒業証書を受け取っているのを見て感動しました。
    Parents were moved to see their children (receiving / received) their diplomas.

［分詞］分詞には、現在分詞と過去分詞があり、名詞を説明する形容詞的な働きをします。現在分詞は動詞の原形＋ ing で表し、「～している」という意味になります。過去分詞は、動詞＋ ed または不規則動詞の場合はそれぞれ異なる形で表し、「～される・～された」という意味になります。

Topic 15: Thank You Messages for ALTs

いろいろな感謝の言葉を学びましょう。

◆ Sentence Match & Chant

 94

以下は、児童からケイティへの感謝の言葉を貼った色紙です。下の日本語に合う英文の番号を入れましょう。次に音声を聞いて練習しましょう。

a. 私たちを教えてくれてありがとうございました。（　　　）
b. 先生の英語の授業は楽しかったです。（　　　）
c. あなたは、すばらしい先生です。（　　　）
d. 会えなくなるとさびしいです。（　　　）
e. 先生と楽しい時間が過ごせました。（　　　）
f. 私たちにしてくれたことすべてに感謝します。（　　　）
g. 私たちは先生が大好きです。（　　　）
h. 英語のゲームが楽しかったです。（　　　）
i. 先生のことを忘れません。（　　　）

UNIT 15: Graduation

Useful Expressions

覚えておきたいフレーズを学びましょう。

◆ Word Order

今年で辞める ALT への感謝の言葉です。単語を並べ替えて文を完成させましょう。

1. この一年、お手伝いいただきありがとうございました。

    Thank _____

    help / your/ for / you

    this school year.

2. あなたと仕事が一緒にできてとても楽しかったです。

    I really _____.

    with / working / you / enjoyed

3. 私たちにしてくださったことすべてに感謝します。

    Thank you for _____

    have / you / everything / done / that

    for us.

4. すばらしい授業をありがとうございました。

    Thank you _____.

    wonderful / your / lessons / for

5. あなたのご協力に感謝します。

    We _____.

    support / your / appreciate / really

6. あなたからたくさんのことを学びました。

    We _____ you.

    lot / from / a / learned

103

児童英語教育の定番教材例―マザーグース・歌、絵本―

■マザーグース（ナーサリーライム）・歌

児童英語教育で広く用いられているマザーグース（ナーサリーライム）と歌（p. 35、p. 41 Column 参照）の例を紹介します。

● *Rain, Rain, Go Away*

Rain, rain, go away, Come again another day,
Little Johnny wants to play, Rain, rain, go away.

「雨、雨、どこかへ行っちゃって。小さなジョニーが遊びたいのだから。」英語圏では雨が降っているときに子どもたちがこのナーサリーライムを歌います。教室でも雨降りのときにみんなで言ってみるとよいでしょう。

● *Apples, Peaches, Pears and Plums*

Apples, peaches, pears and plums,
Tell me when your birthday comes,
January, February, March, April, May, June,
July, August, September, October, November, December.

このナーサリーライムは縄跳び歌としても知られています。大縄で跳ぶときは、自分の誕生月のときに、縄に入ったり出たりします。リズムよく月名を覚える練習になります。

● *Old MacDonald Had a Farm*

「マクドナルドおじいさん」の牧場にはいろいろな動物がいます。鳴き声があちこちで聞こえる、にぎやかで愉快な歌です。英語での動物の鳴き声を知る勉強にもなります。

● *Bingo*

「ビンゴ」は子犬の名前です。最初は B-I-N-G-O と歌い、2回目は B だけ手拍子にして、(手拍子)-I-N-G-O と歌います。1文字ずつ手拍子を増やしていき、6回目は手拍子だけになります。キャンプなどでも楽しく歌える歌です。

■絵本

以下は、広く世界で知られている代表的な絵本の例です。英語のレッスンにもよく使用され、教室での指導用に作られた大きな本（ビッグブック）も販売されています。

● *Brown Bear, Brown Bear, What Do You See?*

「茶色いくまさん、何を見てるの」「赤い鳥が僕を見てるんだよ」と、同じ文章の繰り返しで物語が展開し、色や動物の名前がリズムよく学べます。また、このセンテンス・パターン（構文）を使って、いろいろなアクティビティができます。

● *The Very Hungry Caterpillar*

おなかの空いた青虫が、毎日いろいろなものを食べて大きくなっていきます。食べ過ぎてお腹をこわしますが、葉っぱを食べて元気を取り戻し、成長してさなぎになり、最後にはきれいなチョウになるというお話です。曜日や食べ物の名前が覚えられ、チョウの一生の学習にも使えます。

● *The Gingerbread Man*

クリスマスシーズンによく見られる「クッキー坊や」のお話です。おばあさんがクッキーを焼き、オーブンを開けると「つかまるもんか、僕はジンジャーブレッドマンだぞ」と言って、坊やは家を出て行ってしまいます。最後には坊やは狐にだまされて食べられてしまうというお話です。

小学校では、ALTに出身国の民話などを紹介してもらってもよいでしょう。また、日本の昔話を英語で学習して留学生などに伝えたりできると、物語を通した異文化理解の学習につながります。

文字指導・フォニックス指導

　外国語活動では「聞く」「話す」ことが中心となっていますが、英語が正式な教科となった5・6年生では、十分な音声指導を前提として「読む」「書く」ことが授業に取り入れられています。ここでは、アルファベットとフォニックスの指導の一例を紹介します。

■文字指導の基礎と方法〜アルファベットへの慣れ親しみから〜

　文字学習は、アルファベットに慣れ親しむことから始めましょう。アルファベットは、日本語の文字と全く異なるので、児童が楽しみながら文字に慣れるよう、時間をかけて指導するとよいでしょう。
　まず、歌やチャンツでアルファベットの文字の順番を覚え、文字を認識することが、文字を読み・書きする上で助けとなります。基本表現を使い、カードゲームやパズル、文字探しなどアルファベットの認識を強化するさまざまなアクティビティを行うとよいでしょう。アルファベットをマスターすることは、日本の児童に大きな達成感を与えます。また、アルファベットが言え、書けることで、フォニックス、リーディング、ライティング、その他のアクティビティの幅が大きく広がります。
　児童が文字の読み方に慣れたら、大文字、小文字の順番で4線の上に正確に、丁寧に書けるように指導します。名前の書き方も練習し、提出物には必ず名前を書かせます。学習した単語、英文をノートに写すことで、学んだ英語が再確認できます。与えられた単語を並べ替えたり、例文を部分的に入れ替えたりすれば、自己紹介文や簡単な手紙などが書けるようになります。

■フォニックス（発音とつづりの関係）の指導〜メリットと指導手順〜

　フォニックスとは英語の文字（つづり）と音（発音）の関係を学ぶ、もともとは英語圏の子どものための学習法です。フォニックスを学ぶことで、英語が読みやすくなります。発音とつづりの関係については、これまでは中学校での指導内容でしたが、教科化に際しては、小学校でもアルファベットに「読み方」と「音」があることを認識する活動などが取り入れられることが示されています。なお、フォニックスの指導は、英語の音にたっぷりふれてから始めることが大切です。
　フォニックスのルールを段階的に学び、一つずつ覚えることで、単語や簡単な文章が読めるようになり、文字への興味を高めることも期待されます。ルールを教え込むような指導だと困難を感じる児童も出てきますので、指導には工夫が必要でしょう。指導者には十分な音声学的知識やスキルも求められます。以下は、指導段階の一例です。

1. 「A-Z Phonics Chant（フォニックスチャント）」（右図）でアルファベットの文字と音に慣れる。児童向けにはイラストのあるチャートを使用するようにします。
2. アルファベットの音と文字を認識できる。
3. 短母音を含む簡単な3文字単語が読める。
　例：bat, cat, hat, mat, rat
4. 二文字一音（ch, sh, th）で始まる単語がいくつか言える・読める。　　例：chip, ship, thin, this
5. 長母音＋サイレント e（母音はアルファベットの読み方）
　長母音を含む簡単な単語がいくつか読める。
　例：tape, mate, pine, kite, note, hope

> **A-Z Phonics Chant**（例：言い方は A・[æ]・ant）
> A-ant, B-bag, C-cat, D-dog, E-egg, F-fan, G-gum, H-hat, I-in, J-jet, K-king, L-leg, M-mat, N-net, O-on, P-pig, Q-quiz, R-rat, S-sun, T-ten, U-up, V-vet, W-win, X-fox, Y-yes, Z-zip

　児童英語教育の指導経験から、フォニックスの学習を通して、児童は読む力、書く力の基礎を養うことができると考えられます。フォニックス学習は児童のその後の自律学習の助けになることも期待されます。

※参考資料：
　文字指導やアルファベット文字の認識等の指導のための、文部科学省のワークシートについては以下。
　http://www.mext.go.jp/a_menu/kokusai/gaikokugo/1356183.htm

学校生活に関わる語彙リスト

科目、クラブ名、学校行事など、学校生活に関わりの深い語彙をまとめておきます。本書の学習及び、学校現場でも役立つ内容になっています。ぜひ活用してください。

■ Subjects　科目
活用例：What is your favorite subject? / What subject do you like?　　I like _____.
（Unit 2 p. 19 参照）

• Japanese	国語	• math	算数
• science	理科	• social studies	社会
• English	英語	• music	音楽
• arts and crafts	図工	• home economics	家庭科
• P.E.	体育	• integrated studies	総合的な学習の時間
• life environmental studies	生活科	• calligraphy	書道・書写

■ School Clubs　クラブ活動
活用例：What club are you in?　　I'm in the _____ club.
（Unit 2 p. 19 参照）　　　　　　I'm on the _____ team*.

• cooking	料理	• science	理科
• drama	劇	• music	音楽
• dancing	ダンス	• soccer	サッカー
• ping-pong	ピンポン（卓球）	• softball	ソフトボール
• volleyball	バレーボール	• track and field	陸上
• computer	パソコン	• painting	絵画

＊サッカー、ソフトボール、バレーボールなど、チームを組んで行う競技について言います。

■ Weather　天気
活用例：How is the weather?　　It's _____.
（Unit 5 p. 39 参照）

• sunny	晴れている	• cloudy	くもっている
• rainy	雨が降っている	• snowy	雪が降っている
• windy	風が強い	• stormy	荒れている
• humid	湿気が多い	• muggy	蒸し暑い
• foggy	霧が立ちこめている	• hot	暑い
• warm	（ぽかぽか）暖かい	• cool	涼しい
• cold	寒い	• freezing	凍えるように寒い

■ **The Yearly Schedule / Elementary School Events**　年中行事／小学校の行事
行事の種類や呼び名、行う時期は地域や学校により多少異なります。

活用例：When is the entrance ceremony?　It's in April.
（Unit 13 p. 91 参照）

- entrance ceremony　　　　　入学式
- sports festival　　　　　　　運動会
- field trip　　　　　　　　　遠足
- classroom visit　　　　　　　授業参観
- opening ceremony　　　　　始業式
- closing ceremony　　　　　　終業式
- students' exhibit / arts festival　学芸会
- school concert　　　　　　　音楽会
- school trip / excursion　　　　修学旅行
- [spring / summer / winter] break / vacation / holiday　春／夏／冬休み
- graduation ceremony　　　　卒業式

■ **本書に出てくる語彙（参考）**
学校の教職員・校内（Unit 1）、校庭の遊具（Unit 2）、給食（Unit 3）、遊び（Unit 4）、ほめ言葉（Unit 5）、ゲームの言葉（Unit 6, 7）、振り返りの言葉（Unit 8）、身体の部位（Unit 9）、植物・生物に関する語彙（Unit 10）、調理に関する語彙（Unit 11）、建物・文房具（Unit 12）、折り紙（Unit 13）、避難訓練（Unit 14）、感謝の言葉（Unit 15）

■ **その他の語彙**
子どもへの英語指導に必要な基本的な語彙です。よく復習しておきましょう。

数、月名、曜日、日にち（1st～31st）、時間、色、形、身につけるもの、日常生活に使うもの、食べ物（よく食べる食材、野菜、果物、スナック、飲み物）、動物、植物、職業、国名、形容詞など

覚えておきたい教室英語表現50

　本書で学んだ教室英語と、学校現場で役立つ表現50を厳選しました。英語が言えたら□にチェックを入れます。全てにチェックできるように、繰り返し練習しましょう。

■ ALTとのコミュニケーション
（参考 Unit: 1, 2, 5, 14, 15）

- ☐ **1.** あなたはどこの出身ですか。　　　Where are you from?
- ☐ **2.** 学校へはどうやって来ますか。　　How do you come to school?
- ☐ **3.** あなたを校長先生にご紹介します。　I'd like to introduce you to our principal.
- ☐ **4.** こちらは、5年生の担任の原先生です。　This is Ms. Hara, a fifth grade homeroom teacher.
- ☐ **5.** 校内をご案内しましょう。　　　　I'll show you around our school.
- ☐ **6.** 職員室は1階にあります。　　　　The teachers' office is on the first floor.
- ☐ **7.** コピー機の使い方を教えましょう。　Let me show you how to use the copying machine.
- ☐ **8.** ここが教材の保管場所です。　　　This is where we keep the teaching materials.
- ☐ **9.** 5・6年生は週に2回英語の授業があります。　The students in the fifth and sixth grades have English twice a week.
- ☐ **10.** 8時20分までに学校へ来てください。　Please come to school by 8:20 a.m.
- ☐ **11.** 1時間目は8時50分に始まります。　The first class starts at 8:50 a.m.
- ☐ **12.** 簡単な英語を使って自己紹介をしてください。　Please introduce yourself using simple English.
- ☐ **13.** 火曜日の放課後にミーティングがあります。　We'll have a meeting after school on Tuesdays.
- ☐ **14.** 質問があれば、何でも遠慮なく私に聞いてください。　Please feel free to ask me any questions.
- ☐ **15.** 今日は火災訓練があります。　　　Today we'll have a fire drill.
- ☐ **16.** 担任の先生を手伝ってください。　Please help the homeroom teacher.
- ☐ **17.** あなたと一緒に仕事ができて、とても楽しかったです。　I really enjoyed working with you.
- ☐ **18.** あなたが私たちにしてくださったすべてのことに感謝します。　Thank you for everything that you have done for us.

■児童とのコミュニケーション　～教室で使う言葉・ゲームに使う言葉～
　（参考 Unit: 2, 3, 4, 5, 6, 7, 8, 12）

☐ **19.**	何年生ですか。	What grade are you in?
☐ **20.**	何のクラブに入っていますか。	What club are you in?
☐ **21.**	好きな科目は何ですか。	What is your favorite subject?
☐ **22.**	友達と何をするのが好きですか。	What do you like to do with your friends?
☐ **23.**	兄弟（姉妹）はいますか。	Do you have any brothers or sisters?
☐ **24.**	今日はどんな天気ですか。	How is the weather today?
☐ **25.**	今日は何月何日ですか。	What's the date today?
☐ **26.**	今日は何曜日ですか。	What day is it today?
☐ **27.**	よい週末を過ごしましたか。	Did you have a nice weekend?
☐ **28.**	みなさん、英語の時間ですよ。	Everyone, it's English time.
☐ **29.**	60までの数の復習をしましょう。	Let's review the numbers 1 to 60.
☐ **30.**	数は、とてもよくわかっていますね。	You know the numbers really well.
☐ **31.**	この調子で続けてね。	Keep trying.
☐ **32.**	お昼の時間です。	It's time for lunch.
☐ **33.**	手を洗ってうがいをしてください。	Wash your hands and gargle.
☐ **34.**	給食当番は誰ですか。	Who are the servers of the day?
☐ **35.**	20分休みです。外に出て遊びましょう。	20-minute recess! Let's go out and play.
☐ **36.**	私が鬼ですよ。つかまえますよ。	I'm "it." I'm going to get you.
☐ **37.**	つかまえた。	I got you.
☐ **38.**	あぶない。気をつけてね。	Watch out! Please be careful.
☐ **39.**	太郎、かなを押しましたね。「ごめんなさい」と言いなさい。	Taro, you pushed Kana. Say, "I'm sorry."

- ☐ **40.** グループワーク用に、机を並べてください。   Please arrange the desks for group work.
- ☐ **41.** グループの人と協力して、作業をしなさい。   Work together with the members of your group.
- ☐ **42.** 絵を描いて色を塗り、切り取って地図に貼りなさい。   Draw pictures, color them, cut them out, and paste them on the map.
- ☐ **43.** ゲームをしましょう。   Let's play a game!
- ☐ **44.** カードを上向きにして、ばらばらに並べましょう。   Spread out the cards face up.
- ☐ **45.** 取ったカードを一緒に数えましょう。   Let's count the cards you got together.
- ☐ **46.** 友達と英語を使おうとしましたか。   Did you try to use English with your friends?
- ☐ **47.** 振り返りカードに記入してください。   Please fill in your reflection cards.
- ☐ **48.** 列の前の人にカードを渡してください。   Please pass your cards to the front.
- ☐ **49.** 今日はこれで終わりです。   That's all for today.
- ☐ **50.** 今日は一生懸命がんばりましたね。   You worked hard today.

TEXT PRODUCTION STAFF

edited by	編集	
INOUE, Misako	井上 美佐子	
English-language editing by	英文校閲	
Bill Benfield	ビル・ベンフィールド	
cover design by	表紙デザイン	
in-print	インプリント	
text design by	本文デザイン	
in-print	インプリント	
illustration by	イラスト	
KANO, Rieko	かの りえこ	

CD PRODUCTION STAFF

narrated by	吹き込み者
Carolyn Miller (AmE)	キャロリン・ミラー（アメリカ英語）
Josh Keller (AmE)	ジョシュ・ケラー（アメリカ英語）
Rachel Walzer (AmE)	レイチェル・ワルツァー（アメリカ英語）
Dominic Allen (AmE)	ドミニク・アレン（アメリカ英語）

［編集協力］　大庭裕（元・東京都新宿区立西新宿小学校校長）
　　　　　　東京都小学校英語活動研究会

［音源・音楽提供］　EDUPORT、明石隼汰、HARIO

Hello, English ―English for Teachers of Children―
子どもに教える先生のための英語 ― 会話から授業まで ―

2016年1月20日　初版発行
2024年3月5日　第8刷発行

著　者　　相羽 千州子　　藤原 真知子
　　　　　　Brian Byrd　　Jason Barrows
発行者　　佐野 英一郎
発行所　　株式会社 成美堂
　　　　　〒101-0052　東京都千代田区神田小川町3-22
　　　　　TEL 03-3291-2261　FAX 03-3293-5490
　　　　　https://www.seibido.co.jp

印刷・製本　　倉敷印刷(株)

ISBN 978-4-7919-4797-3　　　　　　　　　　　　　　Printed in Japan

・落丁・乱丁本はお取り替えします。
・本書の無断複写は、著作権上の例外を除き著作権侵害となります。